Buttermilk

Growing Up on a Sandhill Subsistence Farm
in Louisiana during the Great Depression

Thomas Ard Sylvest

authorHOUSE

AuthorHouse™
1663 Liberty Drive
Bloomington, IN 47403
www.authorhouse.com
Phone: 1 (800) 839-8640

© *2015 Thomas Ard Sylvest. All rights reserved.*
Cover art by Thomas Sylvest Jr

Edited by Paul J. Sylvest and Thomas Sylvest, Jr.

No part of this book may be reproduced, stored in a retrieval system, or transmitted by any means without the written permission of the author.

Published by AuthorHouse 12/03/2015

ISBN: 978-1-5049-6603-0 (sc)
ISBN: 978-1-5049-6612-2 (e)

Library of Congress Control Number: 2015919908

Print information available on the last page.

Any people depicted in stock imagery provided by Thinkstock are models, and such images are being used for illustrative purposes only. Certain stock imagery © Thinkstock.

This book is printed on acid-free paper.

Because of the dynamic nature of the Internet, any web addresses or links contained in this book may have changed since publication and may no longer be valid. The views expressed in this work are solely those of the author and do not necessarily reflect the views of the publisher, and the publisher hereby disclaims any responsibility for them.

Table of Contents

Preface vii

Introduction 1

Containers 11

Water Containers 12

Syrup Cans 22

Kitchen Containers 28

Glass Jars and The Cooker 34

General Use Containers for Field and Barnyard 43

Transportation 54

That T & P Train through Provencal 71

Music 87

Provencal High School 104

Open Range	120
Medicine and Health Care	134
The Town of Provencal	147
Soil Conservation	160
Seeds and Plant Propagation	167
Old Blue	182
Building a Log Church	190
Fire in the Piney Woods	197
Author's Timeline	207
Pictures	209

Preface

In my earlier books about growing up on a subsistence farm in Louisiana during the Great Depression, one entitled Collard Greens and the other Cornbread, I recounted mostly from memory stories of events that took place near Provencal, Louisiana in Natchitoches Parish. I began writing these memoirs because my seven children asked me to write down some of the stories I told them of my childhood. After they received some of the stories via e-mail some of my offspring insisted that I collect some of these stories and have then published. The result was Collard Greens, self-published by me through AuthorHouse in 2008.

Collard Greens was well-received. Many folks who enjoyed Collard Greens later asked questions about the conditions of that time and other experiences I had during the Great Depression years, topics I had not included in Collard Greens.

Once again, my children encouraged me to continue writing the stories for the world. And so, I did. The result was my second book, Cornbread, self-published by me at AuthorHouse in 2012.

I am now confronted with the same kind of requests to write more.

We shall see what the resulting product may be. I am calling this third installment Buttermilk.

Thomas Ard Sylvest 2/15/2013

Introduction

A description of the setting within which my stories occurred is warranted. This may help you understand the circumstances of those times in the 1920s and 1930s during the Great Depression.

During the Great Depression, poverty and unemployment represented the most common conditions of people living in the sand hills of Natchitoches Parish. This was true throughout the South including Appalachia. These two economic and social conditions require some explanation.

I learned in fourth-grade Geography that over half of the population of the United States lived under rural conditions in 1930. About 1937, I heard one of Franklin D. Roosevelt's fireside chats over John I. Foshee's radio. I learned that half of the working population was described as unemployed.

What was defined as rural?

My definition is simply what I remember. Rural people did not live in "town." People were rural if they lived where the land available to them was enough for them to engage in growing much of their food and caring for their livestock such as chickens, pigs, cows, and horses. Most of them did not have running water in their homes. Few had electricity.

To me, a common denominator for rural living was the family cow for production of milk and butter consumed at home. If you kept a cow and produced your own milk and butter then you were rural. The inevitable residual of churning cream to make and remove the butter was the buttermilk. Hence, the title of this book, Buttermilk.

If buttermilk was produced by your family, you were rural. However, there was some ambiguity in using this as the definition of rural. Someone could live in town and own or rent land outside of town to keep a milk cow and grow a few crops. At the end of a workday, these folks could return to town after they attended to their "rural" land if it was within walking distance.

Unemployment needs to be more specifically defined also given my experience. The definition used by the government in the twenty-first century is not adequate to define such during the great depression. My definition of an unemployed person was an adult who did not own, or control, and farm his own land and was not paid by someone else for working. This definition leaves some ambiguity about the tenant on a farm.

These definitions would not meet the criterion for inclusion in an economics textbook of today. They are just from my memory of them. Hopefully, they will help you understand what I am trying to write.

Unemployed adults were in poverty and dependent upon someone else for sustenance. So were the members of their families. I knew nothing of wealth as an inheritance.

I did not live near anyone I knew who had inherited a livelihood.

Against this backdrop we can fill in some more blanks to help make a picture. Family units were typically large. Birth control was not common knowledge nor nearly universally accepted and practiced so the number of births was often as high as ten or more per couple. I am number 11 of the 13 children born to my parents, for example. When I grew up our closest neighbor, who was the same age as my father, had 22 children by two wives.

Not all children lived to adulthood in those years. My parents lost three of their thirteen children during their infancy, three years old or less. The evidence of this historic fact and pattern lies in the cemetery at Provencal, the grave marker of my three infant brothers, and other such grave markers in the other cemeteries of our countryside.

One of the reasons for the deaths of children was that our medical scientists had not yet discovered causes nor remedies for common diseases from infections like pneumonia. Penicillin and antibiotics were not in use, and immunization was in its infancy. Disease causes and controls were often just discovered or still not known such as the connection of mosquitoes with yellow fever and malaria.

Transportation was mostly walking, riding on horseback or in wagons. Some long distance travelers used trains and boats. Airplanes were not yet involved in getting members of the public from city to city. Gasoline and diesel powered automobiles and trucks did not join trains in becoming the leading mode of transporting people, goods and munitions until the twentieth century.

Some people were employed in that they were trying to grow food on owned or rented land. Such activity did not produce enough product nor a market for it which could give the worker and his family the additional necessities of life, clothing and shelter.

Some of the economic distress which began during the years immediately before the beginning of the 1930s resulted from the greatest and most devastating flood in the history of the United States known as the flood of

1927. Additional stress occurred with the stock market crash of 1929. The credit and banking systems seemed to cease to function.

To help provide a bit of historic backdrop, Herbert Hoover was elected president in 1929 about the same time as the stock market crash. He served until Franklin Roosevelt was elected in 1933. Some of these basic facts I learned from history at school and not from distinct personal memories of their occurrence. I do remember the election of Mr. Roosevelt.

There was the large surge of people moving from east to west in the United States. This grew from the acquisition of the area covered by the 48 contiguous states, the last one of them, Arizona, having been admitted to the union in 1912.

Many of the rural home sites had been homesteaded between the time of the War Between the States in the 1860s and the beginning of the Great Depression, which designation I simply call the 1930s. Most of the original sites homesteaded had changed hands several times by the

1930s as had the 160 acres purchased in a Section 18 south of Provencal Louisiana in Natchitoches Parish in about 1923 by my father, John D. Sylvest.

A physical feature which helps to visualize the landscape of the 1930s was that nearly all of the timbered land that had not been purchased nor homesteaded by the end of the Nineteenth Century had been purchased by owner-investors from the United States Government for the purpose of cutting and marketing the timber. By about 1930 nearly all of the timber across the South had been cut. Only remnant tracts of timber land remained which contained virgin pine, cypress and hardwood throughout the South.

I recall seeing only one large tract of land, extending for miles in the vicinity of Boyce and Flatwoods, LA. covered with virgin pine timber. "Virgin timber" was the term applied to timber that had been standing uncut for years when the white settlers came to this country. There are only isolated plots of such timber currently remaining uncut in the nation's Southland.

In the vicinity of Provencal and Vowell's Mill, LA. during the 1930s, one had extended views of denuded hillsides. The large virgin trees which had occupied the countryside for hundreds of years were gone. The hillsides were covered with the remaining large pine stumps blackened by forest fires that had burned the tops of the cut virgin trees.

Sailing ships structured of wood were still widely used into the early Twentieth Century. The forest products, known as Naval Stores, constituted primarily of turpentine and its derivatives. These were still in demand domestically and for export. The consequence of that was that pine trees in forests of the South were tapped for turpentine harvested there from prior to cutting the tree and sawing it into lumber.

Many of the present day towns, villages and cities across the South were first founded for the purpose of locating a settlement for workers needed by the sawmills. Some of them are named for the original owners of the mills such as Lutcher, LA., in St. James Parish and Vowell's Mill in

Natchitoches Parish. Some towns were located near the turn of the Nineteenth Century by the railroad which necessarily accompanied a moving population and the huge lumber mills. Such a town is Ruston, LA in Lincoln Parish.

The Sylvest homestead was near both Provencal and Vowell's Mill.

Our statewide museums document that the timber harvest in Louisiana began rapidly in the 1890s. The harvest was largely completed in the 1920s.

I remember that there were barren hills for miles and miles when I was in elementary school in Provencal in the early 1930s. I often walked with friends two or three miles from my home to go to the top of some of the highest hills within miles simply to see how far we could see.

There was a hill about three miles from my home called "Snare Hill," southwest from Provencal and more or less south of Robeline where we visited. It is near the head of Horsepen Creek on the map. From Snare Hill on a clear winter day we could see the smoke coming from the

Sawmill at Peason, LA. approximately 15 miles south of Snare Hill and about ten miles west of Kisatchie, LA. That is nearly a third of the way from Provencal to Leesville, LA. approximately 40 miles. There were other high elevations with clear views for miles. One of those spots was Victoria Hill, also the site of a sawmill at one time. Victoria Hill is about two miles northwest of Provencal. Additionally, there was a fire lookout tower about halfway between Provencal and Robeline. Another fire tower was located near Bellwood, LA.

The rolling sand hills of much of the state, and many of the other states across the South, are like the ones I have described above. As the years passed and forests were replanted or left alone to reseed themselves it was no longer easy to view long distances from hill tops as the new stand of tall dense timber obstructed the views. It is a rewarding memory about which to tell stories of one's childhood.

Maybe you will enjoy the stories too.

Containers

Surviving on the subsistence farm required the use of containers in which to, transport, process and clean produce of all kinds. Everything that we produced had to be put into containers which could be handled by hand.

Water Containers

Our family required vessels for containing water. They included buckets, tubs, and barrels. When I was a child, these vessels were primarily made of wood. In time, we began using galvanized, zinc-coated steel containers. The galvanized containers began appearing in the Provencal area during the 1930s and eventually replaced most of the wooden vessels. The transition from wood containers, tubs, buckets and barrels was gradual. Some of the wood containers, held together by metal straps of copper or steel or by steel wire lasted for fifteen years. Hence, the transition from wood to metal for these purposes, throughout America, lasted from the 1920s until the 1940s, spanning the Great Depression completely. Galvanized containers were used to handle all kinds of produce and liquids. Some examples are cane syrup or cane juice or large quantities of fruits or vegetables. We didn't use the galvanized containers for canning.

As mentioned, we used buckets, tubs and barrels. These containers did the job before pumps, water tanks, pipes, lavatories and faucets.

Water Buckets

The most essential container was a bucket. Before we used the standard 10 quart zinc-coated steel or galvanized bucket, we used buckets made of cedar or oak. Even after we acquired a galvanized bucket, we still used a wooden bucket made of cedar for our drinking water container.

When buckets were used for water, they had two primary purposes, water for consumption and water for hygiene. Certainly we used water for drinking and cooking. We also needed water for bathing and cleaning things like dishes and clothes.

As mentioned earlier, a cedar bucket was our drinking water bucket. It resided on the shelf at the end of the hallway at all times except when it had been emptied. The shelf was called the "water shelf," what else. The water in this bucket came from our well. When it was emptied, we would take the bucket from the water shelf to the well and refill it using our galvanized bucket used to retrieve well water. Typically, every home had a water well, a water shelf and a drinking water bucket.

At our well, one of the zinc-coated buckets was tied permanently to a rope. The rope was threaded through a steel pulley hanging over the opening of the well curb. Sometimes the well rope had a spring loaded steel snap on the end so it could be connected conveniently to a bucket. The metal bucket was lowered to the bottom of a well, fifty feet deep in our yard, where it would tilt over and dip a bucket full of water which was pulled back to the surface with the rope. Our well had a wooden windlass turned by means of a hand crank with which to wind the rope on the drum of the windlass. The drum, made of wood was about

12 inches in diameter and about 24 inches long. The end of the rope opposite the bucket could be seen where it was attached by nails to the windlass drum.

As little children we learned the danger of suddenly releasing the rope as the windlass would allow the rope to unwind and the hand crank would spin and knock a child to the ground as the rope and bucket descended freely to the bottom of the well. Sometimes such an event would damage the windlass or the bucket or entangle the rope, let alone injure the child. That was clearly never to be allowed.

Well Buckets and Rain Barrels

Most of the water we used at the homestead came from the well. However, we also had a wooden rain barrel. The barrel set on the ground under the end of a gutter that ran the fifty foot length of our porch and hallway. The water in the barrel was for ready access to water in case the house caught on fire. The roof of our house caught on fire more than one time when I was growing up and the adults present climbed a ladder with buckets of water and doused the fire until it was put out. A rain barrel for fire water was a standard fixture at homes with wood-burning fireplaces and wood-burning stoves.

The uses made of the well bucket were daily, and many times daily. All the water we used was fetched with the well bucket except for the water collected in the fire-water barrel. However, if the rain was inadequate to fill the fire-water barrel, we completed the filling with well water.

A well bucket could have a small leak in it and still be used for years. The same was not true of the water bucket which set on the water shelf on the porch. In the early 1930s the bucket there was a wooden cedar bucket. Before I finished high school, in 1942, the wood bucket had worn out and disappeared, having been replaced by a galvanized metal bucket.

Not every homestead had a well, so many families acquired their water from a spring sometimes as far away as a quarter of a mile. This is a long, time consuming distance to carry two gallons of water. A gallon of water weighs about 8 1/2 pounds.

Dippers

Other types of water containers that accompanied the water bucket were dippers of various descriptions. One commonly used dipper for community drinking at the Sylvest homestead was a gourd dipper. The gourds from which these dippers were fashioned were grown on the farm. We grew them in the edge of the field instead of the vegetable garden because we did not want them to cross pollinate with our cucumbers, which we grew in our vegetable garden, and make the cucumbers bitter like gourds.

As time progressed through the 1930s steel dippers, often called "tin" dippers, gradually replaced the gourd dippers. These metal dippers had handles about fourteen inches long, the tip end of which was bent into a hook which, when the dipper was submerged in the water in the bucket, the hook on the handle caught on the rim of the bucket and prevented the whole dipper from falling into the water. Different households had their own habits with respect to keeping the dipper available in reach of the water bucket.

Gourd dippers were kept hanging on a limb near a spring of running water along the many trails travelled through the woods. I remember where there were several springs which were running before I was born and had never had their flow interrupted. Sometimes the dipper at the spring hung on a nail on a nearby tree or in the frame which was often built around the spring to keep farm animals from entering the water, thereby keeping it cleaner for drinking.

Wash Pans

Along with the water bucket and dipper on the water shelf a wash pan was kept. A wash pan, porcelain or steel, was about 14 inches in diameter and about six inches deep. It was used to contain water to be used for washing face and hands, especially before each meal. Following the brief, limited bath, the user was expected to throw the water out into the yard. Sometimes next person to use the wash pan had to first throw the water away because the previous user did not.

A bar of soap was kept in a soap dish or some such container for use in washing face and hands. And a bath towel for drying hands and face after washing was kept hanging on a peg or nail nearby.

Wash Tubs

Other galvanized containers used on the Sylvest homestead during the Great Depression were the wash tubs. The tubs which would hold up to about 30 gallons were made of wood like the buckets. However they were also replaced with metal galvanized tubs by the middle of the 1930s. We used two sizes of wash tubs for washing clothes, for bathing, for gathering washing and transporting any farm produce either by hand, on a horse drawn slide or in a wagon.

The galvanized tubs were large enough that they had metal handle on two sides. It required two persons to lift and walk with a tub only about half filled with water, potatoes, corn or any farm produce, crop or food. The larger of the two tubs was known as a Number 3 washtub. The smaller one was known as a Number 2. The Number 2 could hold about 20 gallons. The larger held about 30. The amount of water put into the tub for the current task was carefully judged so that no more than the required amount would be used. The adult drawing the water from the well saw to it that the water drawn was not wasted.

The galvanized tubs were primarily used as bath tubs and wash tubs for cleaning clothes. I recall a disturbed mother when Minnie found that one of her "menfolks," as she referred to male family members, had borrowed one of her wash tubs, as they were called, and had not returned it to her wash benches near the well in our back yard after they used it for some purpose. That was a totally denied freedom. The tubs were Minnie's and no one dared leave them anywhere but in their proper place. I do not recall a second such incident.

I recall these tubs being used for other purposes. For instance, in the field, tubs were good for hauling tomatoes, potatoes, plums, apples, peaches, cantaloupes, grapes, muscadines, blackberries, sweet potatoes, Irish potatoes, peanuts and anything else we grew.

In early winter, it was time to butcher hogs. Tubs were essential to the process whether it was the water to be used or as a container for the meat of the carcass. The tubs were used to catch the waste material by-products of the butchering process. The intestines of as many as five hogs killed on one day constituted a large volume. The undigested food in the intestines had to be washed out and buried to dispose of it. This operation was done a hundred yards, or further, out into the fields surrounding the butchering site. Tubs were used for this purpose.

In addition, the tubs were used for further cleaning of the edible portions to be saved, the chitterlings, which we called, "chitlins" made of the stomach and the large intestines. The sausage casings were made of the small intestines.

Syrup Cans

A handy vessel, for many uses was the syrup can. The common size of the syrup cans held five pounds or ten pounds of cane syrup. Beyond their use as syrup containers, the cans were admirably adapted to preserving seeds of many kinds.

Seeds, when kept during the winter to plant the following year were the favorite food of rodents, rats and mice. So, metal cans, like the tin cans used for syrup protected the seeds well. So did glass jars. Seeds contain living plants and require continuous respiration, metabolism at a low level, to survive and remain viable. They cannot be sealed in containers. The tin syrup cans met this requirement when twenty or so small nail holes were driven into the lids. Before storing the seed in the syrup can the lid of the syrup can was placed on a block of wood (ever present stove wood blocks met the need) and a nail was driven through the lid about twenty times. This amount of aeration kept the seed viable until the following spring, yet the sharp teeth of rodents could not penetrate the metal.

On the surface of this subject it might seem that with a hundred different kinds of seed to preserve it would require a lot of space to store so many cans. Not so, the technique of adequate quantities of the smaller seeds in brown paper bags, frugally saved for this purpose, and writing the name of the seed and the date on the paper bag cataloged the process quite well. A dozen of such small paper wrappings containing small seeds like mustard, collards and turnips could be kept in one metal can.

Minnie would have forty or so kinds of seeds in two syrup cans wrapped in the brown paper, labeled, placed in the syrup can with a list of the seeds contained in the can.

The list was placed neatly on top inside the can. Several cans were used because no prudent homestead manager, which Minnie Sylvest surely was, would put all of the seed she owned of any species in a single container where her only seed existed. Accidents do happen which could destroy your last seed.

Another way of preserving seed was to use a small jelly jar or pickle jar which had a metal lid. Drive the nail holes in the lid and the jar could be used to store the seed.

Improvising in the use of containers was a trade in which instruction began with the observation from the high chair on Sylvest homestead.

Another use of the syrup cans was demonstrated by Minnie one hot summer day when older siblings of the writer had brought all the ingredients necessary for the production of homemade ice-cream in the hand crank freezer.

For one of the Fourth of July celebrations, the young people and grandchildren would get excited at the prospect of ice cream. No sooner was the mix of milk, cream, sugar and flavor put it into the freezer container than the crank on the freezer malfunctioned. No freezer…no ice-cream?

Minnie cautioned her concerned younger offspring not to cry. She then instructed the producers to remove the mixture from the freezer container and pour it into a syrup can. She put the lid on the can and put the can into the ice-cream freezer tub surrounded with the ice, water, salt mixture.

She further instructed, "Now, hold the wire bail of the can in your hand and twist the can clockwise and counterclockwise, alternately."

Within fifteen minutes the party was eating homemade ice-cream made without a hand-crank freezer. Not as smooth a product as with the hand-crank machine with a dasher, but good enough to reward everyone, especially the apprentice seated in the highchair nearby.

Honestly, I do not remember being seated in the high chair that day but I never forgot the lessons. Lessons? Yes: 1. "Don't cry over spilled milk" 2. "All's well that ends well." 3. "There is more than one way of doing most any job." The list is endless. That names only a few of the lessons learned or reinforced. Many more could be added to the list and the multiple opportunities these "mishaps" provided for Minnie to teach seemed to be endless.

One knowledgeable lady! I think the observer in the high chair was benefiting from what Minnie had learned while raising the older siblings. Don't tell anyone. It is a secret. But I had these lessons once learned many times reinforced by listening to those esteemed older brothers and sisters.

An open topped ceramic container shaped like a barrel with a capacity of about 8 quarts, a ceramic lid with a one inch round hole in the middle, edges tapered so the lid would fit into the ring molded into the rim of the container, a wood paddle made by fastening with a wood screw two five inch crossed boards 1 1/4 inches wide and 1/2 inch thick into the shape of a cross, mitered to fit on the end of a 24 inch round handle one inch in diameter:

What was that just described by that apprenticed occupant of that high chair? It was Minnie's churn, of course; and the dasher.

From thence came, not only the best butter in Natchitoches Parish, and the most delicious buttermilk I ever tasted, so good it would make fresh cracklin' cornbread all but melt in your mouth. And here is the source of the title of this volume. All of this from the kingbird seat in the high chair makes up the book, Buttermilk.

Kitchen Containers

Dish Pans and Enameled Containers

A fine example of a multi-functional kitchen container is the dish pan. It was the largest container that was normally used on the cook table and counter. In the early 1930s, the dish pans were mostly made with steel coated with baked on enamel. They were also called "granite" dish pans. That material was used at the time for many other utensils such as coffee pots, smaller pans, and sauce pans for cooking. The dishpan and similar smaller pans were used to prepare produce for cooking. The dish pan itself met the need of a container in which to gather and shell peas, butter beans and snap beans or green beans. The vegetables which produced a lot of trimmings and was voluminous like the hulls of peas or beans, or peelings of potatoes called for the large container. Sometimes even the Number 2 washtub was used to contain a load of fruit or vegetables being prepared for cooking or preserving. The dishpans were about twelve quarts in capacity and somewhat shallow. When it was placed in your lap filled with beans to snap, your hands could reach the produce without your forearm bearing on the sides of a deep pot, a very uncomfortable and tiring position.

Most homes in the piney woods had more than one dishpan, and often had three or more. Those that had become so banged up, bent or had cracked porcelain, even though they might leak, were still treasured for their utility because they remained valuable for gathering produce and transporting it to the kitchen or other destination. We did not use the "good dishpan" for uses where they were likely to get abused, saving the one that did not yet leak for the princess assignments of the kitchen, such as making biscuits. A profound truth is here to be learned;

do not abuse your best on the more menial assignments. Similarly, save your best clothes for going to church and special occasions.

The enameled containers of smaller and deeper design were used like the dishpans to prepare produce. Additionally, they were used for cooking food on the top of the wood burning stove. Most of these intermediate sized containers of one or two gallons had lids so heat was not lost during cooking.

An interesting problem with enameled coated steel containers was the tendency for the enamel to chip off. When the enamel chipped off such as it did around the bottom edge of the pan, the steel remaining was susceptible to rusting and springing a leak. When a pot or pan leaked it could no longer be used for cooking. However, such damaged pots or pans were not thrown away. The general merchandise stores sold a small package of different sized patches. These patches could be installed in a hole with gaskets and washers protecting a tiny connecting bolt which went through the hole and a washer with nut placed on it. After the patch was bolted into place with the miniature bolt, nut and wrench, the metal of the patch was pressed or bent into the contour of the container. Such a package of patches was commonly called a package of "Mendits." I do not recall who the manufacturer of the patches was nor if the name was just a trade name. I do recall buying them at Harry Hawthorne's general merchandise store in Provencal. I also recall that my mother bought some from Pete Holland who peddled Watkin's products throughout the Provencal, Vowell's Mill and Bellwood areas of our part of the woods in Natchitoches Parish.

Cast Iron

Cast iron containers were and are still used worldwide for cooking. Among the kitchen containers we had was a black cast iron kettle. We used it for heating water either in the fireplace or on the wood stove. This kettle held about ten quarts. If you heated the kettle full of water to boiling and poured it into one of the washtubs it required about two 10-quart buckets of ambient temperature well water to cool the water to bath temperature.

Containers for cooking were anchored by two sizes of cast iron skillets, pots, and a five-quart Dutch oven. The cast iron skillets were handy for many food preparations. They were particularly preferred when baking cornbread as the more desirable thicker crust resulted. I still use two such skillets for this purpose.

The Dutch oven was versatile for cooking in the fireplace, on top of the stove, in the oven or on the bank of a creek outdoors. It had a cast iron lid so it could be used for frying, boiling or baking in many settings.

Standard kitchen equipment also included one or two additional deep cast iron pots of about six quarts capacity. These were used for cooking casserole type dishes such as beans, peas and some other vegetables. Some of these pots had steel legs attached. Most of them did not.

Baking Tins

Baking tins both rectangular and round for all kinds of baking were present in every homestead kitchen. From these came cakes, pies, bread, and biscuits that would make your mouth water.

One staple daily food, cornbread, was usually cooked in the cast iron skillets. However, it was sometimes cooked in rectangular steel baking tins or in cake and pie tins. The same was the case for baking biscuits.

Ceramic Dishes

Kitchen containers for storing food such as leftovers were primarily ceramic dishes which were used for serving dishes as well. At the end of each meal the leftover food was consolidated in the serving dishes, placed on shelves inside screened cabinets called "safes." Food thus protected from insects and rodents was then available for eating between meals or for serving at the next meal.

Glass Jars and The Cooker

Not to be considered the least among the less important kitchen containers were glass fruit jars. Fruit jars of all sizes, from half pints to gallon jugs. And all of them were sized to be sealed with Mason fruit jar lids. We used these glass jars to contain all manner of preserved foods. The preserving process was called "canning." This was true notwithstanding the fact that the containers were made of glass and not metal. Hundreds of jars were used during the summer and autumn when produce was plentiful. During the winter months, home-canned food was a mainstay when fresh vegetables and fruit were scarce.

A special container called a "cooker," an enameled metal pot about 10 inches deep and 20 inches in diameter, was essential to the preserving process. We used the cooker to sterilize glass jars and their contents for later use. About six one-quart jars could be sterilized in the cooker at once. In this manner the preserving process could complete many jars in one day.

There were limits to how many jars could be used and how much preserving could be done in one day. For instance, one determinant was the amount of produce available. For example, if we wished to can 50 quarts of butter beans, the row of butter beans in our garden did not produce enough beans at one time to fill more than a few jars. So, some jars would be filled the next week when more beans were available.

Another limitation on how much produce could be canned in one day was labor. It was a labor intensive process. The household members could only find time to prepare certain amounts of produce in a single day. Other routine tasks of the homestead still had to be performed. So available time and labor were limitations.

Certain crops, such as the root crops, like carrots, and beets could sometimes be canned in quantity in one day as large portions of the crop matured at one time. Such was often the case with large fruit trees such as apples, peaches or pears or an orchard of smaller trees like plums.

The cooker was a valuable cooking pot. Sometimes, if many neighbors were present to eat, the cooker would be used to cook a large quantity of a dish like soup, beans or stew for consumption at the time. Often a goat would be butchered for such an occasion.

The cooker had a tight fitting lid but it was not a pressurized vessel.

Ceramic Containers

Another material that was used to make kitchen type containers was thick ceramic. Ceramic bowls, jugs and pots were common in kitchens at that time. Some of the large containers made of this material were used in preserving meats of all kinds. A ceramic container of about ten gallons capacity was used to marinate meat for smoking.

Smaller bowls made of the thick ceramic were used as milk containers and serving bowls.

We referred to vessels made of this material as crockery as it was manufactured as pottery.

Some of the crock type ceramic material was used to make special purpose containers such as the churn in which my mother churned sour cream to make butter. This container was shaped like a miniature barrel. It had a ceramic cover with a hole about one inch in diameter in the center. A round wood handle about 3/4 inches in diameter had two small paddles attached to one end of the handle in the shape of a cross. The handle was inserted into the hole in the lid above which the handle protruded about 10 inches. This extension of the handle enabled the operator to move the handle up and down about six inches once per second churning the contents until the butter coagulated.

Two interesting and rewarding products resulted from this churning process, butter and buttermilk. The third portion was whey, which, rich in protein, was fed to animals, particularly chickens and hogs.

Miscellaneous Kitchen Type Containers

Drinking glasses were obtained from our neighbors. Several of the Foshee families who lived nearby had household members who used snuff. Probably close to fifty percent of the adults of the community used snuff. Since an 8 ounce snuff container had a metal cover which was fastened to the glass by the glued on label the clean clear glass container was a household treasure on the homesteads in the piney woods. All glasses were carefully preserved. I know my mother often arranged with the neighbors that she would exchange something like butter or eggs for drinking glasses. From these we drank beverages at meal time, milk, buttermilk or water.

For hot beverages like coffee or chocolate the drinking utensil of choice was a ceramic cup or coffee cup sometimes accompanied by a saucer, sometimes not.

Lard cans and syrup cans and other rare metal containers were retained after they were emptied of their original contents. Lard cans came in several sizes generally called four pound lard cans, 8 pound lard cans and 48 pound lard cans. We did not purchase lard nor shortening in these cans, as we raised pigs and produced our own lard. Occasionally we obtained such used containers from neighbors and preserved carefully every container whatsoever.

Syrup cans were the tin cans of about three and one-half quart capacity manufactured to be used to put homemade cane syrup in to store or sell. We sold some of the syrup. The cans left empty from syrup we had consumed were carefully preserved for re-use as syrup or as general containers. The size of the cans was manufactured to hold exactly ten pounds of cane syrup. There was a less common size which held half that amount, five pounds of syrup.

Flour sacks made of cotton cloth and brown paper bags met some occasional needs for containers. Several items purchased at general merchandise stores came in brown paper bags. The clerk serving the customer chose a brown paper bag of the right size to hold the quantity of the merchandise ordered. Skilled at his/her trade, the clerk was often the store owner or his wife or descendant. White sugar, green coffee and ground coffee were the most common purchases packaged in brown paper bags. Dry beans and peas were also sold and delivered to the customer in the brown paper bags.

To execute the purchase the clerk took the verbal order, selected the right size paper bag, opened the bag, and set it on a scale which resided permanently on the counter. The sugar was dipped from a large container nearby with a scoop and poured into the bag on the scale until the reading of the weight was for the ordered amount. The process was the same for many other items such as beans, peas, rice, etc.

The brown paper bags were temporary containers. Woe to the customer who walked home with brown paper bags full of something like sugar and got caught in the rain. For this reason the customer usually reserved items that were purchased in brown paper for acquisition when a vehicle was available to haul it that offered weather protection. Such was not always an available option; the purchaser had to watch the weather.

The flour and corn meal were pre-package in 24 or 48 pound cloth bags, not in the variety of many fancy paper or plastic packages of the twenty-first century. As we grew our own corn for consumption and feed, we did not often purchase a cloth bag of corn meal. All of these cloth bags were carefully washed and ironed after they were empty as they were to be used for many things. Some cloth bags which came with flour in them were made of print material. So were some sacks which contained feed for animals. We usually grew all of our feed consumed by our livestock. Sometimes we purchased feed. Some feed came in the cotton material and some feed came in brown burlap bags

The cloth was suitable for use as quilt linings or for bed sheets. Cloth from bags was also suitable for making garments. Many times the purchaser of a few sacks of feed involved selecting sacks of a certain print pattern so a new dress or shirt could be made for a household member. If several sacks of the same print pattern could be obtained, it facilitated making larger garments such as a dresses, blouses or shirts.

When World War II began in 1941 the USA had already modified the industry so that items needed for war by our allies was being produced. This caused adjustments and changes in some parts of our society and that of other countries. Our textile mills switched over to producing materials for uniforms. This change caused shortages of cotton material suitable for sewing garments. One solution adapted by the war production authorities was to encourage feed manufacturers to use cotton print as sacks to contain feed as it could be used again in sewing garments. Such practices were carried on throughout the nearly five years the USA was engaged directly in World War II. The stage for this effort was set in the 1930s. The war ended in 1945. Japan finally surrendered in August of 1945.

General Use Containers for Field and Barnyard

Wood barrels for water containers, woven baskets for handling produce, and used burlap feed sacks were treasured across the countryside.

Most of our wood barrels came from the Coca Cola Bottling Company which had a plant in Natchitoches during the 1930s. The syrup for making bottled drinks came in the 55 gallon wood barrels. Emptied barrels were discarded. We had acquired several of these barrels. Some were cut in half with a hand saw making two wooden tubs out of one barrel. Such half-barrels were handy for use as washtubs or tubs in which to cure meat.

Some of the barrels were kept as they were when procured for later use as cane syrup containers. These were filled with homemade cane syrup. For years we kept one on a wood rack under our house. It had a bung hole through which it had been filled with syrup. It also had a spigot from which we could drain the syrup. As the syrup was ready for consumption upon removal from the barrel, we simply drew it off one syrup can at a time. One gallon of cane syrup would last our household up to a week.

Sacks and bags of paper, cotton cloth, burlap and canvas met many general needs. Paper bags salvaged from their role as temporary containers to bring purchases home were saved for future use. For example, a mess of turnips from the garden could be put into a large brown paper bag to be carried home by a neighbor whose turnips had not yet come into production. The bag was a one-way container. It was temporary and did not have to be returned. Burlap sacks and flour sacks were expected to be returned. A child's school lunch could be put in a small brown paper bag.

As the smaller brown paper bags were of thinner material, the smallest ones met a special need. Cigarette smokers of the neighborhood often, and typically, could not afford the special papers sold for the purpose of rolling your own cigarettes. The material of choice was the small brown paper bags which could be torn into small bits about two inches by two and one-half inches in size and used to roll Country Gentleman, Bull Durham or even home grown tobacco into a cigarette. I remember seeing one neighbor who smoked pull a piece of paper bag out of his shirt pocket, crumple a torn piece until it was soft and pliable, and pull a bag of Bull Durham smoking tobacco from his shirt pocket. He held the piece of brown paper in his left hand in the shape of a "v", dumped the tobacco from the white cloth bag into the paper, grabbed the cardboard tab on the drawstring of the cotton tobacco bag between his lips, and drew the top of the bag until it was closed. He returned the bag to his shirt pocket with his right hand still holding the tobacco loaded paper in his left hand and then used the fingers of both hands to complete the rolling of the tobacco in the paper. He raised the rolled paper to his mouth, licked the edge of the brown paper with saliva, held the finished product out for examination, and licked the seam once more to insure adequate saliva for sealing in the tobacco. He reached for a "strike anywhere" match from his pocket, turned his bare foot toughened from years of going barefooted, struck the match on the calloused bottom of his foot, lit the cigarette hanging between his lips, and inhaled a long drag, blowing circles of blue smoke from mouth and nostrils as he relished the flavor of the tobacco in the cigarette rolled by his own hands in brown paper.

Interesting facts surrounding the above process include the difference in the sizes of the Bull Durham and Country Gentlemen smoking tobacco containers. The Bull Durham bag was smaller than the Country Gentleman bag so it fit into the dress shirt pocket. For this reason it was more convenient. The Country Gentleman bag, while made to the same pattern, was about twice as large. Packed tightly with smoking tobacco, it was said to hold precisely enough to fill a pint jar if it were packed tightly into the jar. The tobacco in the Bull Durham bag was cut into finer pieces. Because the shredded leaves of tobacco were cut into smaller pieces, the contents were loose and the ash on the end of the cigarette was more likely to fall off and burn your shirt than was the Country Gentleman tobacco.

I observed, as a child, that most pipe smokers said they preferred the Country Gentleman because it packed more securely into the bowls of their pipes.

The cotton muslin Country Gentleman drawstring tobacco sacks were prized by the marble shooting champions of the time as marble containers. Don Mims was the undisputed marble champion attending Provencal High School when I entered high school in 1939. Pat Landry and Leon Bates were competent in the skill of marble shooting.

Cotton Sacks

Sacks of heavy cotton canvas material were used for picking cotton. They could be purchased as ready-made cotton-picking sacks or the material could be purchased and the buyer could fashion his own sacks. The material was tough. It needed to be. The sacks were dragged up and down between the cotton rows as the picker who wore it separated the cotton lint and seed from the cotton boles on two adjacent rows each pass across the field.

A good picker could pick about two hundred pounds of seed cotton per day in the better fields of cotton in the fields of the hill country. In the lands along the rivers of the South, the richer soil of the floodplains and river deltas produced much more cotton per acre and a good picker might be able to pick twice as many pounds of cotton in a day. As an aside, an eight hour day had not yet been invented. The work day for picking cotton day was from "Can to Can't," from the time in the morning that it was light enough for you to see how to pick cotton until it was too dark to see how to pick in the evening.

These canvas cotton picking sacks could be used to contain green forage such as sweet potato vines to bring to farm animals for feed. I used them to haul leaves from the yard when a child. Cotton sacks were stored in the cotton house, a special shed for storing seed cotton after it was picked and until it was ginned.

Burlap Sacks

Burlap was a versatile material. The usual source of burlap was the salvaging of sacks which had come to the homestead filled with feed of some kind, such as cottonseed meal, corn chops, oats, potatoes, or rice. The material was strong and flexible. The bags were typically retained for multiple uses. I remember being sent to the corn crib to get a burlap sack from a stack which was regularly kept there. They were valuable containers which could be used indoors or out. Because the burlap sacks were more weather-resistant they were stored in the corn crib, unlike the brown paper bags which came apart when they got wet and needed to be stored in the kitchen.

Burlap bags were used to package produce like Irish potatoes and sweet potatoes for sale or barter. They substituted for a saddle blanket. Sometimes they were used as a substitute for a saddle, particularly for children. Riding bareback was not the most comfortable way to travel.

The most novel and sobering use to which I ever saw burlap adapted was when a black neighbor in need came to the Sylvest homestead and told my dad he had nothing to feed his family. They were starving. Accompanying the begging man was some of his children including his daughter about 11 years old who was visibly wearing one piece of clothing only, a burlap bag with a hole cut in it so it would slip over the head and two holes cut into it for the arms. It is time to point out that burlap against the skin is exceedingly rough and uncomfortable. This episode has stayed infallibly in my memory.

Burlap was strong enough to be used to repair harnesses for use on draft animals. It was often used especially to make back bands to hold up trace chains used on mules pulling plows.

The bags, typically a bushel or more in capacity, were sometimes opened and restitched by hand into smaller sacks used for carrying a dozen ears of corn to feed hogs in the woods. The small haversack type bag could be suspended by a shoulder strap so your hands were free while mounted to control the reins or handle a gun or ropes and throw ears of corn as feed to hogs. Or the sack was often hung on the horn of the saddle from the shoulder strap.

These bags were also used to carry small game like rabbits, squirrels and birds. They served well as utility containers for occasional use such as gathering wild nuts, chinquapins, hickory nuts or pecans.

Burlap sacks were typically used to contain cottonseed which was returned to the farmer who owned them. The following year when the seed were planted, the sacks became available and were used for myriad uses on the farm.

Cottonseed meal also typically came to the farm in burlap sacks which likewise were retained for many uses.

Woven Baskets

Wood baskets were woven locally by several of our neighbors. The baskets made of white oak or hickory strips of wood about an inch wide. They were widely used in handling cotton. People called them "cotton baskets" though they were used for a variety of other purposes as well. The small homestead sized places throughout the South were sometimes referred to as cotton farms. Most of them along with the large cotton plantations used cotton baskets as cotton containers. The basket had a rigid form and would hold about fifty pounds of cotton when it was stuffed full.

Several of our neighbors made these white oak cotton baskets. The names I can recall from the 1930s who were said to make them were Ellis Honeycutt, Willie Foshee and Jessie Gibbs. It seemed to me that over half the homeowners made cotton baskets. I never saw one being fabricated.

We did not weave our own baskets on the Sylvest homestead. We kept about three at all times to use in handling and loading cotton primarily. We also used them for other things like forage and trash. I can recall being instructed to climb into the cotton house and fill the basket full of seed cotton. The full basket was then handled by an adult outside the cotton house standing on the ground. The basket was handed up to another adult on the cotton truck where it was emptied. The empty basket was handed back into the cotton house for refilling.

Transportation

Getting from place to place on the globe was limited to primitive means up until the nineteenth century. During the 1800s steam power began to be harnessed more widely throughout the world to meet the needs of people. Prior to that time most of the population of the world lived close to rivers and oceans so boats and ships propelled by oars and sails could be used to travel and haul. Overland travel and transportation was primarily by walking, riding horses, and loading pack animals and carts and wagons. Donkeys, camels and elephants were used in some parts of the world. Oxen were often the draft animals available for pulling plows or wheeled vehicles. So, it is in comparatively recent time that more rapid movement of people and goods has occurred.

Steam-powered boats really only came into common use in the Nineteenth Century. That is the century in which my father was born near Franklinton, LA., on February 18, 1879. He was raised in a log cabin which is on the National Historic Register and is preserved in the Mile Branch Settlement on the Washington Parish Fairgrounds at Franklinton, about 80 miles north of New Orleans.

Few people living today in the United States of America can even begin to imagine there not being millions of people in automobiles, on buses, trains and airplanes riding and flying daily all over the globe within hours. For this reason I write about transportation, not as a specific chronological and scientific history but as an elder conveying a sketch of the past to his children as he recalls it.

The living octogenarian of the present can only describe from an awestruck view of the rapid changes in transportation he has experienced in his lifetime.

Bluntly, in summary, it was during the American Civil War that steam power came into its own as the means of moving large numbers of people and large amounts of goods over this nation and in Europe and crossing the ocean in between. Steam-powered locomotives and steam-powered boats and ships were the conveyances that were just beginning to be capable of accomplishing this demand for rapid mass movement of people and goods. Following the Civil War, the first railroad across the USA was completed.

Today coal, oil, and gas-powered generating plants still produce the bulk of the world's electricity by making and using steam. A small percentage comes from hydroelectric plants and an even smaller percentage comes from solar power. Even the sometimes controversial nuclear generating plants producing electricity use steam in the process of converting nuclear power into electricity. The radioactive fuel of the nuclear plants merely provides the heat to convert water into steam. These same principles apply to the large ocean going vessels. Each consumes some kind of fuel to produce the steam to convert into electricity which then propels the vessel.

Replacing ox carts and wagons was difficult. Using steam to propel these proved impractical. This persisted until the three decades before the Great Depression.

A steam engine needed to be proportionally small enough for a cart, wagon, or tractor. However, it needed a constant supply of water to make the steam. This proved very difficult, though some efforts were directed towards this early on. Boats didn't have this problem because there was the ever available water for making steam. Locomotives had supplies of water at regular intervals along the rails. A constant demand for water when crossing dry plains or desert made powering wagons or ox carts with steam impractical.

The solution to this impracticality turned out to be the internal combustion engine for both stationary and mobile use. Enter gasoline and diesel as the agents of choice. To this day, the internal combustion engine is the king in this arena.

Where does this fit into my memoirs of growing up in the sand hills of Louisiana during the Great Depression? Stay tuned for the story.

I certainly could not see the barns where our horses and mules were kept when I was born in 1925. The horses, mules and other farm animals were kept in stables, pens and pastures away from the house we lived in because of the foul odors of the barnyard. So our barnyard was located a hundred yards or more away from the dwelling. This was a typical homestead arrangement of the time.

The location of dwelling versus barnyard involved more than distance. Drinking water sources and sanitation were considerations as well. No homestead situated these facilities so the drainage from the barnyard was through the yard of the dwelling or the well, stream or spring supplying drinking water.

From the high chair I could see the front yard fence made of pickets with a gate with a weighted closing device attached. Our front yard gate had a self latching bar which automatically latched the gate when it was closed. To insure that the gate would not be left open, the closing device pulled the gate closed unless the person who when through the gate blocked the gate in some manner. The closing device is made by attaching a chain or rope to the top of the gate at the closing end of the gate. The other end of the rope was fastened to a stake about 30 degrees out of line with the fence and about ten feet away from the closing edge of the gate. A weight, such as two bricks or some such heavy object, was put on the closing rope so it would cause the closing device to pull the gate until the automatic latch fastened.

A child sitting in a high chair for two or three years, much of the time on the porch with a wide open field of view learned about the gate, the fence, the animals that passed by, the ever present yard dog, and the mouser. Every farm had one or more house cats. One of these typically lived in the house part of the time and the rest of the time lived mostly at the barnyard.

This high chair individual had ample opportunity to observe the gate closing device as well as other attractions.

The child watched the maintenance and repairs of all this which took place daily, as needed.

One obvious observation was about the transportation. Rarely does anyone leave the house or yard unless they are walking. Only a few times per day or week does the observer see any member of the household or a visitor approach or depart on a mule or horse. Much more seldom than that does this young observer see the team of mules hitched to the wagon and one or more members of his family depart in the wagon on some trip. Ninety percent of those occurrences were only to haul something from one place to another on the homestead.

For a time this high chair observer was me. Other children had their turns in the high chair. I was learning for the first three years or so of my life, 1925 through 1928, at an awesome rate. Not only did I know how to whistle, but I knew the names of all the members of the household, sometimes numbering ten or more. Further, I knew the names of the mules and horses and the dog and cows. Besides, I had a pet goat, all my own, named

Billy, which I was allowed to raise on a bottle as, for some reason, he was motherless. I remember feeding him as he grew larger at a much faster rate than I. My older brothers and sisters were afraid the goat was going to hurt me as he hurled himself with all his might in the direction of the nipple on that bottle of milk. They taught me to give Billy the bottle through the cracks in the fence so he would not butt me accidentally or purposely injure me.

Seldom did a vehicle appear on the wagon road which lead from La Hwy. 117 for nine-tenths of a mile to our house, nor on the wide expanse in front of our home outside the yard gate. That area covered more than an acre and was called the "stomp" where cattle, mostly ours, assembled there each evening and often slept there at night. That area was devoid of grass and was hard packed soil as the feet of the cattle kept the area denuded.

Sometimes the members of the house would saddle a mule and tie her to the fence outside the gate. I was getting more and more interested in transportation of the time. Every time another member of the household older than

I left the house I wanted to accompany them. I was often allowed to go with them if they were walking. That was most of the time. However, getting on a mule or in a wagon appealed to me a great deal more. High chair occupants have great difficulty with patience. It takes a while to grow large enough to be allowed to ride a mule.

Sometimes, the opportunity came along for me to go with my mother when she rode in the wagon. That was mostly on Sunday mornings, when the weather permitted. John D. would have one of my older brothers harness the mules and hitch them to the wagon because Minnie and the high chair members of the household, my younger sister, Ruth Germaine, and I, were going to ride the five miles to Bellwood Baptist Church to Sunday School and church services.

I remember my mom putting a couple of quilts, old ones, not her best, in the wagon. When we two younger ones (referred to in common speech of the time as "younguns") got sleepy, we were placed on the quilts to sleep. Now the suspensions on those wooden wheeled wagons with the steel rims on the wheels were not as soft as those of your twenty-first century automobile. When your head was on the floor of that wagon with only a quilt between it and the wood and the wheel of that wagon rolled over a tree root about three inches in diameter in the middle of the wagon road, you felt it. I do know that sometimes we slept that way. Now, I do not understand how. Not only did tree roots interfere with a smooth ride, but the noisy ride on the graveled portion of the road made a harsh sound like no other as the iron tires on the wheels crushed gravel for five miles of the ten-mile roundtrip.

How can the former high chair supervisor remember all this? One must ask the more legitimate question: how could he ever forget?

That was my introduction to the transportation of the 1920s.

More lessons about transportation in the world remained for me to learn. Under the protection of barn and shed roofs on our homestead were two Model "T" Ford vehicles, a truck and a two seater passenger vehicle. I never saw either of them run. When I started to school in 1931 they had not been cranked in five years because there was no money to buy gasoline.

So the children of the family, including me, grew up not learning how to drive an automobile. This same scenario was played out on hundreds of such homesteads throughout the South and commonly in the rest of the rural portion of the country.

The rubber tires on the vehicles parked at the Sylvest homestead rotted off while I was growing up to age 6, the age to start to school. The economic situation on the homestead did not improve much for about ten more years.

So, what was going on in the field of transportation in the rest of the world in the first four decades of the twentieth century?

Oxen were pretty much being phased out for general movement of people. Most family vehicles were still pulled by horses and mules into the 1920s. Thousands upon thousands of mules and horses were shipped to Europe to be used in the cavalry, artillery and as pack animals for our military and the military of our allies.

The personal experience that enables me to state that in my memoirs is that I had dozens of contacts with World War I uncles, relatives and neighbors, who told me so. Then, as the Great Depression turned into World War II in 1940 through 1942, I observed the horse cavalry executing maneuvers in the Kisatchie National Forest in Natchitoches Parish Louisiana with Dwight Eisenhower and George Patton, leading WW II Generals, as two of the generals in charge at the time. During those maneuvers I observed artillery, large guns being drawn by horses. I recall opening our field gate and letting a mounted soldier enter our farm to go hide from the enemy with whom the mock battle maneuvers was taking place. That was on the Sylvest homestead about 1941.

Tanks had been better developed by 1941, just before the attack on Pearl Harbor on December 7, 1941. The number of heavy duty trucks, gasoline powered and half-tracks for pulling artillery guns were rapidly replacing horse-drawn vehicles. It was that recent by my own witness. I observed all of this before I finished high school in June 1942 at age 16.

In 1942 we were still using Springfield Model 1903, 22 caliber rifles for training and practice in the Louisiana State University Reserve Officer Training Corps in which I enrolled at age 16. We used the 22 caliber weapons in our training because that was all that was available. The USA still had not been able to shift to wartime production of equipment and ammunitions at a level to send all the rifles needed by our allies in Europe and had not been able to produce enough ammunition to keep the U. S. Marines supplied with adequate ammunition to defend themselves on the islands of the Pacific Theater of Operations after the beginning of World War II.

Shifting from the so-called "horse and buggy" days into a mechanized economy and armed forces could not be made in a year or two. It took from December 7, 1941 when the Japanese bombed Pearl Harbor until the end of the war with Japan in August of 1945 to accomplish most of that transition in the military only.

The railroads throughout the United States were strained to the breaking point during WW II because they were the primary means our population used to move from place to place.

Why had not internal combustion engines for automobiles made up the difference by 1945?

IF NO ONE HAS TOLD YOU AT HOME NOR IN YOUR HISTORY BOOKS, NO AUTOMOBILES WERE MANUFACTURED IN THE USA FOR FIVE YEARS DURING WW II. THERE ARE NO ANTIQUE 1942, 1943, 1944, NOR 1945 AUTOMOBILES BECAUSE NONE WERE MADE. THE SAME APPLIES TO TRUCKS; NONE WERE MANUFACTURED FOR CIVILIAN USE DURING THOSE YEARS.

This is a good point in my story to make the point that a war is not a picnic.

It was largely after WWII that the manufacturing facilities of the USA included diesel-powered trucks, the forerunners of our current 18 wheelers.

At the end of WW II, in 1945, 18 wheelers would have been ahead of their time. There were not yet enough paved roads in the USA to handle the volume of traffic that would have been needed. The paved roads in existence were too narrow and were built to accommodate vehicles of the 1920s. The heavy trucks in use delivering merchandise and hauling produce in the area of the piney woods were trucks of less than 100 horsepower with only ten wheels and not 18. They were primarily fueled by gasoline and not diesel. The first diesel engines I saw were mostly stationary in power sawmills, electric generating plants, and pumps, though I did see boats and buses powered by diesel.

Moving numbers of passengers had been limited to railroads to this time. However, as production of vehicles other than for military use increased during the two decades following WW II, the shorter railroad routes which were carrying primarily passengers began to disappear.

It takes time for such major changes to be made. Roads were being improved and hard surfaced as fast as federal, state and local governments could pay for them.

Under President Eisenhower (1953 to 1961) our transportation infrastructure began to grow. Interstate highways came into being. These facilitated the movement of goods in particular and improvements in the trucking industry. As diesel powered trucks increased, steam locomotives declined. Railroads did not disappear, but diesel locomotives slowly replaced the steam ones.

While these changes were taking place over the decades following WW II, more passenger planes were produced and the age of air travel had begun. There was a crop dusting company in Monroe, LA that began flying passengers as early as the late 1930s. It grew and became Delta Airlines. At least one major airline originated in Louisiana.

From this backdrop the transportation of people and goods over the world moved from the residual of horse and buggy days of the early 1900s gradually to automobiles and then to air travel within about fifty years. The Wright Brothers flying machine and gasoline powered vehicles began around 1900 and the airlines were hauling many passengers fifty years later in the 1950s.

Similar changes were taking place around the world.

With this story of the development of our current transportation system as a backdrop, I hope it is easier for the reader to keep other developments in perspective.

The daily service provided to Provencal and its surrounding area by the Texas and Pacific Railroad in the 1930s ended around the 1950s. Automobiles had substantially replaced trains as the individual means of transportation.

It was in the 1920s that the phrase, "A car in every garage and a chicken in every pot" came into being, rightly or wrongly, having been attributed to Huey P. Long, then governor of Louisiana.

That T & P Train through Provencal

The local transportation which was in place in Provencal in 1923 was limited to the gravel road which was under construction from Hagewood to Leesville, a distance of approximately fifty miles. Hagewood is five miles north of Provencal on Louisiana Highway 6. The road leading south out of Hagewood was designated as LA Highway 39 when I started to school in 1931, and now appears on maps as Louisiana Highway 117. It was completed as an "improved gravel road" between 1923 and 1931, which construction required several years. I do not know precisely when it was completed. Transportation from community to community in the local vicinity was still largely by horse drawn vehicles. Roads for wagons still followed traditional routes across bridges, often with an alternate fording crossing near the site of the bridge, but not always, over streams like Provencal Bayou, McKim's Creek, Horsepen Creek, Middle Creek, Santa Burb(sp) Creek (name possibly Anglicized from the Spanish "Saint y Barb"), Bayou de Muse and Kisatchie Bayou (also referred to as Kisatchie Creek). These community roads, trails and bridges were built by cooperative effort of neighbors, not part of any official governing body and/or the travelers themselves. A wagon road across a homesteader's property was basically the responsibility of the owner of the property, but not exclusively.

I can recall arriving at a spot on McKims Creek with my dad on a wagon. The ford was down such steep banks that John D. stopped the team and wagon, unhitched the team from the wagon and drove the team across the creek. Then the wagon was pulled into a position by hand where it could be allowed to roll slowly down the bank. One wheel was tied with a rope so it would not turn, thus retarding the speed with which the wagon went down into the creek. After the wagon was in the ford, the wheel was untied. A rope was fastened to the tongue of the wagon and the mule team hitched to the rope. The team slowly pulled the wagon up the sloped bank until the wagon was clear of the slope. The team was then re-hitched to the wagon and the journey was continued. Such improvisations were the daily norm for crossing streams in those times.

The improvisations in all cases were modified to suit different conditions. Actually, a redundancy perhaps? That was the case by definition.

One alternative that often could be applied was the unloading of the wagon so parts of the load could be carried across the creek by hand, boat or whatever, and reloaded on the wagon on the other side of the stream.

When Highway 39 was completed it had a standardized bridge over each stream including the above named. The foundations for the new bridges were made of heavy creosote treated sills and lumber. Boards of the bridge deck were about three inches thick by a nominal twelve inches wide. Cracks about a half inch wide were left between the boards decking the bridge. This allowed for drainage of rain water away from the wood to avoid hastened decay.

Prior to the construction of Highway 39, the roads were simply the routes that wagons had used to go from Vowells Mill to Provencal, from Shady Grove to Shake Hat, from Bellwood to Fort Jessup, from Kisatchie to Cypress, from Flora to Provencal, from Natchitoches to Provencal, from Lotus to Kisatchie, from Provencal to Robeline, etc.

Just this year, 2013, I was asked by a host how long it had been since I had been over the road from Natchitoches through the hills by Collin's Nursery to Provencal.

I replied, "Approximately sixty years."

My host said, "We'll go over it now." Sixty years ago that route was an old unimproved wagon road about ten miles in length.

Then, there was a wagon road still in use in nearly any direction anyone wished to go for a distance of a few miles.

I rode from the Sylvest homestead on a wagon to locations on various points of the compass between 1925, the year I was born, and about 1935, the nominal middle of the Great Depression. Some of these trips took me to Flora, Vowell's Mill, Bellwood, Shady Grove, and Harmony. Often one of these trips would be routed through the woods on an old wagon road, over old bridges and sometimes required the removal of downed trees which had fallen into the right-of-way. Another segment of the trip was often routes along Highway 117 or 476 or any of the designations used to identify the additional improved roads that grew up connecting various communities. A man traveling even a few miles with a team and wagon often carried a crosscut saw and an ax or sometimes two axes to be available for removing obstructions or rerouting around deep holes.

Gradually, during the 1930s the wagon roads were used less and less. Each of them I travelled as a child provides fond memories for me. As wagons traveled at a slow pace, perhaps 2 to 3 miles per hour, there was ample time available to traveling children to learn about the natural springs of water along these roads, the bridges, and the configuration of the streams as they flowed under the bridges.

Sometimes the bridges were in a state of ill repair and required at least minimal repairs before the team and wagon could safely cross. Teams of mules sometimes could not be forced to go over bridges they deemed unsafe, no matter what their driver thought.

I remember driving in a wagon through the piney woods from the Sylvest homestead to Harmony Church to a church service. After the church service we drove to the residence of Jimmie Roberts. The home of Mr. Roberts was located close to the banks of McKims Creek. From the house of Mr. Roberts a wagon road led west, crossing McKims Creek over a community bridge. Our team objected to crossing the McKims Creek Bridge at that point. However, after some masterful mule management by John D., possibly blind-folding the one balky mule that was the most recalcitrant and leading the team across the bridge, on this occasion the crossing was safely made and our route then led us past the homestead of Steve Roberts, later to become the property of Jefferson Masters and his wife, Jane Honeycutt Masters. The route led from the Steve Roberts' place west to cross Highway 39, across Corral Branch, and past the homestead of one of our black neighbors, Andrew Lynch and his son, John Lynch, and John's wife, Beulah McGaskey Lynch.

John and Beulah Lynch had small children, the eldest of which was my playmate and my age. He was named John D. Lynch after my father. Mrs. Lynch often helped my mother who was ill much of my early childhood.

From the Lynch place on that that wagon road we traveled west another mile past the Wade place, later acquired by Meade and Mary Ann Miller of Provencal. From the Wade place to the Sylvest homestead was only another half mile. This trip took an entire day, from shortly after daybreak until near sundown.

That was quite a wagon trip with a family. I recall that Loree Roberts, daughter of Mr. and Mrs. Jimmie Roberts, was present the day of our visit. Loree attended Provencal

High School with me though she was a year or two older than I.

I can still picture the visit to the Jimmie Roberts place where we ate the noon meal called "dinner," our visit an hour or two after dinner and the crossing of the McKims Creek bridge with the reluctant team of mules, Jane and Pearl.

The old wagon roads disappeared by about 1940. The bridges by that time had decomposed.

The route from Vowell's Mill to Provencal was one of the older ones in the community. It continued in limited use for decades after the depression. Finally, it is no longer maintained as an alternate route as a bridge across Horsepen Creek is impassable.

There were homesteads along each side of that road which departed from LA Highway 39 just a mile south of Provencal and led southwest for about 8 miles across Horsepen Creek, and Bayou de Muse on the way. In the 1930s at the Vowell's Mill end of that route was a school building plus a filling station and general store. It seems to me that the businesses belonged to a man named John Canady, a community leader in the area.

I do not recall seeing any remnants of a sawmill near Vowell's Mill. Some mills were loaded on the trains and hauled away after the targeted tracts of timber had been cut.

The surrounding lands had been purchased by investors around 1895, the mills constructed, the turpentine bled from the pine trees, and the virgin timber, some of the trees over 500 years old cut and sawed into lumber.

By 1931, about the earliest time I could remember, there were no longer any virgin pine trees uncut. The surrounding countryside was an endless scene of rolling hillsides covered by stumps of pine trees, blackened by fires that burned periodically as uncontrolled woods fires or forest fires, if a forest were present. Local citizens were permitted by law to allow their livestock, cows, horses, pigs and goats to range freely and graze over this rather barren landscape of grass and the new undergrowth, the pine forest slowly regenerating itself.

Some of the cutover land belonged to small landowners, most of whom had long ago sold the timber or had acquired their land after the timber had been cut, as in the case of the Sylvest homestead. However, most of the land belonged to large landowners who were referred to as "lumber companies" as many owned sawmills for the purpose of cutting the timber on the land owned by that company.

In the early 1930s the second growth timber had grown back. Local sawmills began custom sawing and even participated in the acquisition, hauling, sawing into lumber, and planing. This occurred even as the large sawmills of the 1920s were ceasing operations, removing their railroads and mills, laying off their workforce, and abandoning their sites.

This countryside of wagon roads, a veritable network that provided a route nearly anywhere, was extended by the presence of the Texas and Pacific Railroad. T&P traversed the countryside from Alexandria and Shreveport with depots and stops every five miles or so along the route. The route led through Provencal.

The passenger train schedule was for an early morning departure from Alexandria, LA arriving at Provencal about 9:15 am. The return trip was an early afternoon departure from Shreveport arriving in Provencal about 3:00 pm. This was just about the time the school buses departed from the school at the end of the school day.

I remember standing on the stiles one day about 1940 and watching a school bus headed south on LA 117 loaded with school children. The bus and the train arrived at the crossing at about the same time. The train was blowing its whistle to high heaven but the bus driver was unaware of the train and rolled across the road only a split second before the train had passed the road. All of the bystanders breathed together a sigh of relief when no collision occurred.

The railroad was not only a route for the passenger and mail train. There were freight trains that passed through daily, dropping off mostly empty boxcars or gondolas which would be left on sidetracks near the depot. They were filled with forest products like piling which were peeled pine poles of various lengths and diameters. Piling and smaller diameter peeled poles were shipped to the creosoting plants such as the one in Colfax, LA. In recent years creosote has been labeled a hazardous material and is not as widely used as it was in the 1930s. Other forest products included cross ties to be used in repairing the railroads, pulpwood for the production of paper and saw logs which were taken to sawmills for sawing into lumber.

As the freight trains arrived, dropped off railcars and pulled others away, the school children were able to observe all the activities associated with the operation of the trains and their cargo.

I recall standing at the wire fence around the school yard and watching the loading activity. Piling were pulled up ramps by rolling them up a ramp of heavy poles called skids. The piling was pulled by a team of large draft animals, mules or horses. When it rolled over the edge of the railcar, the chain released it and the heavy piling, often weighing half a ton, would land in the railcar with a resounding boom. Some schooldays were filled with these booms every few minutes the entire school day. As there was no air-conditioning the large windows were left open for ventilation except on cold days.

Another interesting timber loading job was cross ties. As they were hewed with axes into rectangular shapes of about the same dimensions they were stacked neatly by hand into the railcars. The process of getting the 200 pound crosstie into the rail car was hard work. Typically a long ramp of heave lumber about three inches thick and about twelve inches wide were arranged into a walkway on a sharp incline up which the man carrying a crosstie walked up the ramp with the tie on his shoulder. Only large strong individuals ever tackled that demanding work.

Saw logs were loaded using the same log skids and chains as for pilings. Logs were loaded by a team of draft animals pulling the logs one at a time up a ramp of long poles with a chain. The team was on the opposite side of the railcar from the pile of logs being loaded. So, a driver near the team had a helper who worked on the other side of the railcar for the purpose of pulling the chains back to re-hook them on to the next log to be loaded. The teamster stayed with his team and executed the pull whenever his partner in the loading process indicated that the hitch was ready to pull the load. The "Get Up" command was heard and the load began to move. When the boom ended the pull, the "Whoa" command to stop the team was heard and the whole process began all over again.

Pulpwood trucks usually pulled up to the side of the railcar to be loaded so the loader could toss the pieces of pulpwood one at a time into the railcar.

Sometimes a boxcar was placed on the extra tracks alongside the mail track. These side tracks were called sidings sometimes. They could contain something a family had ordered from a mail order house which required shipment by freight. Examples of these items were cook stoves or agricultural implements.

The amount of freight that arrived for unloading declined sharply during the span covered by my Provencal

High School years. By 1942 furniture and agricultural implements were nearly all being delivered by large trucks. Such trucks were even used by the railroads so they could continue to compete for the countryside freight business by delivering freight from the train or depot to the homestead several miles away.

In the 1940s it was common for locals to get a ticket from the ticket agent at Provencal and ride to Alexandria or to Shreveport. Sometimes the round trip could be made in the same day with a good bit of shopping done at the end of the line.

This practice did not solve the transportation dilemma of the citizenry of the countryside because the homesteader who could arrange for transportation to the depot probably was an automobile owner, or a neighbor to one, or had an offspring who would help with transportation often.

The age of the automobile was on its way, depression or no depression. Early automobile owners were school teachers, who, with an auto did not have to board within walking distance of the school. That was about the time when School Boards no longer were required to have a suitable residence in order to hire a principal because the principal could live in one town and drive to teach in another.

Changes in transportation and needs for transportation took place for many reasons such as all the timber being cut. However, because transportation for individuals and families was changing too, these changes came together without it being clear wherein lay the cause or the effect.

Change was on its way.

Music

Memoirs do not require the expertise and research required to do a scientific treatment of a topic. A superficial artistic presentation of the subject or even a novel requires more knowledge than recollections.

Music in my life began with my being surrounded by a musically talented family. My mother played the piano at church and at home. Seven of her ten children who lived to adulthood learned to play the piano. My five sisters played well enough that they sometimes stayed with a leading church member of surrounding communities like Vowells Mill, Harmony, Bellwood, or Provencal for the length of a one-week revival meeting to play a pump organ or piano for the church services. All ten of us sang in local quartets and church choirs.

My earliest memories of music are of my mother singing to me as she rocked me before I was large enough to graduate to the high chair. Some of her songs were: "Little Red Bird In A Tree" and a little song that told a sad tale in "Three Babes In The Woods." They are classics which you can find on the Internet.

I told you early in this chapter that this is not a classical music lesson. Instead, it is simply some of what I remember.

Recorded music, a new invention, began to reach some of the country homes of the piney woods in the early 1930s on wax records. These could be played on spring loaded windup record players. Then, the battery radio began to creep into the homes of the region.

I had an older brother, Frances Emmanuel Sylvest, named after both of his paternal great grandfathers and who we called, "Frankie," for short. By the time Frankie completed high school, he had acquired a Silvertone guitar from Sears Roebuck and was singing Jimmy Rodgers songs, Gene Autry songs and other traditional country dance songs for dances held in local homes from Vowells Mill to Kisatchie, Bellwood and Provencal. Many of these functions were simply held in homes.

As the 1930s came along, the home music presentation of the record player called the "Victrola," a windup instrument which played songs recorded on thick wax records, transformed the world of country music. Cowboy songs by Slim Whitman and Montana Slim became familiar to me. Before my voice changed at the usual age, I could yodel like Jimmy Rodgers, the singing brakeman. After my voice changed I could still yodel and as I grew up to care for the livestock, I regaled them with all of the country and cowboy tunes I had ever heard. They also heard all the gospel songs that I had ever heard.

By the time I started to school in 1931, or shortly thereafter, I was well attracted to the local country music performers even though I was not able to attend their presentations at the Provencal High School auditorium. There would have been Bob Wills and his Texas Playboys.

That band had to have played in every high school auditorium in Louisiana and East Texas. Ernest Tubb made a hit with "Walking the Floor Over You" with his ever popular off-key song presentation. Jimmie Davis and his Sunshine Boys performed all over the tri-state region of Arkansas, Louisiana and Texas as well as Hollywood for the movies. Jimmy Davis, a school teacher, from Jackson Parish was also a musician, who became Governor of the State of Louisiana and a movie star. He was a personal friend of Dixie Sylvest Moss, my oldest sister.

Bill Monroe entered the country music scene with Blue Grass that was heavily infused with the sounds of mandolin and banjo in addition to the guitar and fiddle. New developments in the music world were taking place rapidly. A few battery-powered radios began to appear in the piney woods, fifteen or twenty years before electricity would finally follow in the early 1950s, in many cases, such as at the Sylvest homestead.

A local country music singer and songwriter, Bill Nettles from Provencal, LA where I attended school played for local dances and concerts. One of the songs he wrote was "Hadacol Boogie." Another song he wrote was "That Poor Potter Boy from Provencal." The latter was a song about a young man named Potter who was shot in an ambush and killed on the Harmony Road near Provencal when I was a school child. Recently, when I searched Mr. Nettles out on the Internet, I observed that he was listed as having been from Monroe, LA. Well, I reasoned, I will let that small matter go as he probably moved there from Provencal so he could play live in Monroe, LA near the broadcasting rooms of KNOE, an early radio station in Monroe. I listened to KNOE and KWKH at every opportunity. I know about the Provencal bit in the Bill Nettles story because when I was in the first grade in 1931 Bill Nettles, Jr., son of the songwriter in question, and resident of the Happy Hollow subdivision, near the Provencal Creek on the South edge of town next to LA Hwy. 117, (then La Hwy. 39) bopped me on the jaw, on the schoolyard with his fist, and I went shamelessly crying to tell my first grade teacher, Blanche McElwee about it.

I do recall that my assailant, Master Bill Nettles, Jr. did not enter second grade with me so I suspect he moved to Monroe about that time with his family. That would have been the summer of 1932.

There were a few other AM radio stations that came on the air in Louisiana in the late 1920s and early 1930s about the same time, KALB in Alexandria, WWL in New Orleans billed as a 50,000 watt clear channel station, and not the least of them all, a country music promoting station in Shreveport, Louisiana called KWKH. I grew up with the story that the station in Shreveport was named after its owner, Mr. W. K. Henderson, hence the name K for the FCC identification as a station west of the Mississippi River followed by WKH, the initials of the presumed first owner. I never verified that story, just remember it with pleasure. I remember hearing Mr. Henderson announce programs on KWKH radio. The Henderson family is still involved in ownership of media facilities in the Shreveport, Louisiana area.

Years before the names "Grand Ole Opry" or "Louisiana Hayride" identified radio shows, country music was being heard on these and other stations such as Del Rio Texas, WOAI San Antonio, WCKY Cincinnati, WSM in Nashville and a station whose call letters I cannot remember in Des Moines, Iowa. I listened to any and all of these stations at every opportunity. Most popular programs in the piney woods were "The Carter Family, " of which June Carter, Johnny Cash's wife was a member. Several gospel groups were popular. I remember one gospel quartet we enjoyed was "The Stamps Quartet." I believe they were from Arkansas. Gospel music on the radio in the late twenties and early thirties was mostly four part quartets. Sometimes a trio, or duet, would perform and, rarely, a church choir would be heard.

The quartet gospel format was also popular at the local singing conventions of the time as well. I remember that the Roberts family, which included Rev. Monroe Roberts, Rev. Oliver Roberts, Oscar Roberts, William Roberts and Steve Roberts often contributed one or more members to the local quartets. I remember that Monroe and Oliver sometimes led singing in the churches they pastored or preached in. Oscar sometimes played the piano or the organ.

To me, nothing exceeded the "All Day Singing and Dinner On The Ground Functions" at the various churches throughout the piney woods region. I loved the music and the appetite of a growing boy, which can never be satisfied, fared heavenly at "All Day Singings and Dinner on the Grounds."

I was visiting in the Vowell's Mill and Provencal region recently and heard of the singing groups in which Mary Ann Miller, of Provencal and my late friend, Robert Singletary, originally of Vowell's Mill, participated in. Singletary was a schoolmate and playmate of mine. While in the piney woods on that trip I enjoyed some of Steve and Minnie Slaughter's cracklin cornbread and collard greens. Minnie Masters Slaughter was named after my mother, Minnie Fendlason Sylvest. Such food and such hospitality is unexcelled. Thank you, Steve and Minnie.

One problem we had at the John I. Foshee house where Weuell, Jewel and I listened to the Carter family regularly was keeping enough sharp phonograph needles. We used to hold the dull needles with a pair of pliers in one hand and a file in the other as we sharpened them with a file, the same files our dads used to sharpen our hoes. These files were usually six, eight or ten inch flat bastard files, files of a medium cut between coarse and second cut. They were about the only kind of files we commonly found around our homesteads.

About 1935 the matter of getting access to a radio to listen to, in addition to wind-up record players, was easing just a bit. I do not recall the year but at least by 1937 Henry McGaskey had a radio. Henry was our closest neighbor, a black man and son of a former slave, who lived only a quarter of a mile from us. We could listen to it with the McGaskey family in the evening on Saturday to hear the news on KWKH in Shreveport. The source of the battery power was Oscar McGaskey's pulpwood truck. Oscar would put his dad's run down radio battery in the pulpwood truck on Sunday evening and park the truck on the hillside from which he could push the standard shift truck off and as it rolled down the grade let the clutch out and crank the engine.

Oscar would drive the truck all week and on Friday night he would remove the dead battery from the radio, exchange it for the charged battery in the truck and repeat the process.

More and more music was coming to the piney woods.

Not only did we hear the country tunes and folksongs we were hearing the cowboy songs and church music. There were enough radios powered by batteries that most everyone occasionally visited at one or more homes that had a radio. Culture was on it's way.

It was about 1935 that the Natchitoches Parish School Board added a visiting teacher of music to their offerings. Dixie Sylvest Moss, my oldest sibling, was that music teacher. I believe the following year an additional visiting music teacher was added.

About the mid-thirties we began to hear the occasional hit parade program. The musical tastes "improved" to the point that some guitar and fiddle music lovers could enjoy a bit of brass band music. Just about then the early beginnings of the big bands including the trumpets of Harry James and violins of Glenn Miller's band began to catch on.

Recording technology was developing rapidly. Amplification improved records greatly.

My oldest sister, Dixie Sylvest, graduated from high school at Louisiana College in 1923. She enrolled in Louisiana State Normal Teachers College in Natchitoches. In 1924, with a temporary teachers certificate she began teaching school at Bellwood Elementary school in Bellwood, LA. Sometime in the 1930s, I believe, it was 1936, she changed jobs with the Natchitoches Parish School Board. She became the first ever "roving" music teacher in Natchitoches Parish. Dixie had studied music along with her education studies which enabled her to teach music. Her music teaching job required her to teach at alternate schools on different days of the week. About 1931 Dixie married Walter Moss, Jr. before becoming the music teacher so she was then known as Mrs. Dixie Moss. She often played the organ at Bellwood Baptist Church. That church building is still standing in 2013. Mrs. Moss died in 2008 at the age of 102.

During the 1930s the number of automobiles on the roads in the piney woods of the South began to increase. The improvement in transportation made it possible for musical performers to extend their range. A country band could load into a station wagon or panel truck and play in Alexandria, LA. one night and in Shreveport La the next.

One of the early local bands was headed by Jimmie Davis, who wrote, "You Are My Sunshine." Jimmie Davis and his Sunshine Boys was a popular band during the Great Depression. He came from Jackson Parish near Jonesboro, LA, about an hour's drive from where I was born. Davis and my sister were both teachers and were close friends during the Great Depression.

I heard Jimmie Davis and the Sunshine Boys playing music at Provencal High School. I still enjoy listening to the voice of Jimmie Davis singing "There's a Mansion, Just Over the Hilltops." He sang and recorded cowboy songs, country music songs, gospel songs and popular songs.

The above exposure to music with the practice I got leading singing at churches gave me a sensitivity to music which still rewards me as I go from country, to gospel, to folk music, to rock, to popular, to classic with an appreciation across the entire field. In later years, I was a song leader at my parish church for many years.

I did attend functions at St. Joseph's Cathedral in Baton Rouge where my niece, daughter of Dixie Moss, was the second organist on perhaps the best organ in the city of Baton Rouge. Edna Beth Moss Finkelstein had her Master's Degree in music from Louisiana State University.

As the "Hit Parade" came along in the mid-1930s, even though radios were scarce, the popular songs began to be sung in the piney woods and were sung by children on the school transfer from Vowells Mill and Bellwood to

Provencal High School. I rode those routes to school from 1935 until I graduated in 1942.

I well remember Letha Lee Kay singing "You Promised Me Love" on our school bus on the way to school. Letha Lee graduated about 1937. This background of music led to love for the same so our gospel music heritage sustained us until further exposure to radio and juke boxes bridged the gap all the way to Mozart and Pavorotti.

No claim to fame myself in the field of music, Eloise, my wife took piano as a child. We still have her piano in our Gramercy, LA living room. Our three daughter's took piano and learned to play on that same instrument.

Our seven children provided the music for the weddings of all seven. Of the seven children, all of them have participated in the choirs and groups who played music in their respective churches. Five of them still participate each Sunday in the liturgies of their respective home churches.

That occasions me to give thanks for the commitment to exposure of our children to basic music that their mother carried out in their growing up years.

My son, Patrick is a professional songwriter and performer although he still maintains that his vocation is as a Certified Registered Nurse Anesthetist who gives anesthesia to patients for surgery in Houma, Louisiana five days a week. He has found time to work on his third album in the studios of Randy Walsh in Bayou Goula, Louisiana. Patrick's first album, "A Little Less Louisiana," was produced in Nashville and may be purchased on the internet. Just search for Patrick Sylvest Music for that and other music he has recorded.

Our oldest, Tommy Sylvest, plays the guitar and has written songs and in 2014 played an engagement at Phil Brady's in Baton Rouge, Louisiana. He lives in Baton Rouge.

John Sylvest, our second child who plays the guitar and has written some songs, is not currently engaged in music pursuits, lives in Baton Rouge. For years he led youth choirs at USL and LSU while in college. He often played for weekend student retreats. John founded a series of student retreats called "Awakenings," which were held at ULL, LSU, and Tulane University.

Our oldest daughter, Mary Margaret Sylvest Folse, is a vocalist, guitar player and pianist. She still gives piano and guitar lessons at her home in Plaquemine, Louisiana and participates in the music ministry where she attends church.

Our middle child, Catherine Sylvest Schaff, of Gramercy, Louisiana teaches piano and is pianist for her church choir.

Our youngest daughter, Teresa Sylvest Dershak, plays the flute and has learned the harp. She frequently plays at her church and for residents of nursing homes.

Finally, our youngest son, Paul Sylvest, leads the music ministry where he attends church in Thibodaux, Louisiana.

The next generation continues the musical heritage with Nicholas Schaff, a grandson, a keyboard player who also plays in some local bands and an army band with which he went overseas to Iraq.

Caroline Schaff, Nicholas' younger sister, majors in creative writing at LSU and writes songs and keeps YouTube busy.

Mathew Sylvest, Patrick's son, a vocalist, who performs with several local bands plays the stand-up bass and doubles with his dad on mandolin and guitar.

Music was an important part of the piney woods experience during the Great Depression.

Looking back, it is not a bad way to get a start.

Provencal High School

Public schools in Louisiana just came into being in the early 1900s. When Dixie and Artie, my two oldest siblings, reached age 6 my parents were working frantically to get a school going near Franklinton in the Bethel Baptist Church community. That was in 1912, 1913 and 1914. By 1914 the school was operating. I do not know if it was a public school. I think an aunt of mine was a teacher at that school, one of John D.'s sisters, possibly.

As more children arrived in that Sylvest household near Franklinton, Dixie and Artie were exhausting the educational resources at the local school and were ready to move on. John D. and Minnie held a family school conference and decided to move to Pineville, LA where a Baptist School was being organized and was subsequently built and became Louisiana College. That school, as did many schools of the time, offered a high school curriculum as well as college courses.

John D. worked as a contractor constructing parts of the buildings of the school, the residences of the faculty, and community at large. He further worked at Camp Beauregard, which was built nearby, as World War I came along about 1917.

World War I ended on November 11, 1918. The years that followed were filled with unemployed veterans and a decline in the general economic activity of the nation as a whole. The piney woods area of Louisiana, in which Louisiana College is located, was not exempt from these difficult economic times.

John D. decided to buy the Sylvest homestead near Provencal from Sam Tarver, which he did in 1923. He did this in order to be able to grow food for his growing family and to gain an environment where parents could control the activities and companionships of their children, especially the juvenile males (no tongue in cheek). The homestead was admirably suited to the control of activities and companionships of the children, especially the cotton patch portion of it. It kept the growing and extended family well fed consistently over the years with, perhaps surprisingly, almost a total absence of cash money. I can assure you that John D. cared about feeding and providing guidance for his offspring a lot more than he cared for whether he had cash in his pocket. As long as he had a few plugs of Brown's Mule chewing tobacco on hand, plus a pound of coffee in the pantry he knew he could produce the rest. He did.

Minnie could spare enough from her supply of egg money to keep him in tobacco and coffee in a pinch, even if she was deficient in money for postage stamps and kerosene, two items not as critical to John D. as to Minnie.

Once I remember, that exact crisis seemed to be descending upon the establishment. About to be a deficiency of money for Brown's Mule? No real sweat.

Dad said, "Son, go over to Mr. John I. Foshee's and get me a few tobacco plants."

Off I went and six months later, with eyes popping out, I watched and helped John D. harvest and cure the tobacco he produced, enough to supply him for a year. We twisted it into hunks which had a remarkable resemblance to a popular twist chewing tobacco brand on the market then called "Hickory Twist."

Subsistence farming may have been the term applied to our situation by the U. S. D. A. Agricultural Economists. I assure you that term would have offended John D. Sylvest immensely.

Let's just face it. He was successful in reaching "his" goals and he knew it.

Dixie graduated from high school at Louisiana College in 1923, the same year of the move to Provencal. Her six siblings were Artie, Vince, Johnnie, Frank, Spurgeon and Pauline. John D. and Minnie had three more children born at Provencal, Ard, Ruth and Royce. Dixie's nine brothers and sisters all attended and graduated from Provencal

High School. One might think that having nine children graduate from Provencal High School was a record. I believe that the Goins family had more and I believe the P. G. and Lottie Kay family probably had more, not to exclude other families because this information is from my memory and not from records. I did not nor do I presently have access to the school records.

The 1920s at Provencal saw the construction of the three-story, all brick high school building in 1927 which continued to be used until about the mid 1940s. Up until 1927, the high school building was a frame building located a few blocks west of the eventual brick high school building (See picture in Pictures and Maps). For about fifteen years after the new building was occupied, the gymnasium of the former frame school was still used by the high school athletes.

When the 1927 school building was built, a well was drilled on the western edge of the school site. A pressure tank was connected to the well output in such a way that when the water pressure dropped to a certain level the power to the pump was turned on to refill the tank. Drinking fountains were located on each of the floors of the three story building. Running water in a school building in a small town in the piney woods? Who ever heard of such a thing? I am not aware of the facts surrounding the power sources for such a convenience. I am aware that the toilets flushed when I started to school in 1931. I believe the setup to have been a Delco Electrical Plant where direct current electricity was provided to batteries which in turn provided at least minimal electric current for lights in the ceilings of hallways and classrooms and in the auditorium including footlights for the stage. I do not recall ever seeing a plugin electrical appliance at Provencal High School.

A word about sanitary facilities is required when describing a school built in 1927.

Classes were daytime functions and any kind of night time activities were limited and seldom. The disposal of wastes was by septic tanks. What a step upward this "new" school is? Running water instead of a well with a bucket, or a pitcher pump, flush toilets with septic tanks instead of open pit outhouses and Provencal school was on an upward climb.

I could not speak as knowledgeably about the levels of instruction, but the physical facilities of the 1930s were quite an improvement over those of the early 1920s.

Schools continued to gain attention in Louisiana as the state began to furnish school transfers (buses). I saw a picture of one which was identified to me as the first gasoline powered school transfer used at Provencal. The date shown on the picture was 1923. During the early 1920s my older siblings rode to school, first in a covered wagon and then in a buggy John D. acquired for that purpose. Roads were still so poor that motorized vehicles had difficulty traversing them. So, many children continued to ride in covered wagons at least part of their way to school. I rode the one mile from Sylvest homestead to LA Hwy 39 (currently La Hwy 117) in a covered wagon driven by John I Foshee. That was probably in 1941. To my knowledge, that was the last covered wagon to haul children, at least part of the distance to Provencal High School.

An interesting aside was that John I. had only one draft animal, a mule. So he arranged with Eric Miller, my first cousin, who owned a mule to borrow the mule so he would have two mules to pull the school wagon. I recall that the name of the mule owned by Mr. Miller was "Lou." Lou had a dished face which gave her a curious appearance and made the entire piece of equipment an object of curiosity. It was a curiosity even to those of us who rode the vehicle daily. This arrangement continued for only one semester as the Police Jury and The School Board cooperated in their effort to provide a passable route down Sylvest Road by adding gravel to muddy spots. As I recall, Mr. Doss Foshee resumed driving his school bus to pick up the children of the area in 1942.

Free textbooks came along, I believe, in the late 1920s when Huey Long was Governor of Louisiana.

In 1931, the year I started to school we were provided textbooks but not pencils, paper, ink, pens and erasers. I remember that there was a rough paper pencil tablet with the picture of an Indian chief on it and the name "BIG CHIEF" printed on it. These were available at the local general merchandise and grocery stores. For use with ink there was what we called the "slick" paper. One of the ink tablets was called "BLUE HORSE" and had a picture of a blue horse on front of the tablet. There were Blue Horse notebooks as well as packages of "slick" paper, intended for use with ink, wrapped in a sheet of paper decorated with the Blue Horse trade symbol.

Three ring binders were available at the local stores as well. Often the teacher of one grade would specify that each student should use a certain tablet or notebook, so all were alike.

There were what we called "penny pencils." The penny pencils did not come with a large eraser fastened on by a metal clamp. They only had a bit of rubber shoved into the top end of the pencil. The lead was hard and the eraser did not last long. These pencils sold for one cent, hence the name. Larger yellow pencils with an eraser on one end were available at local stores at a price of two for a nickel. Each pencil had an eraser which was the diameter of the pencil and the eraser was attached by being clamped to the end of the pencil with metal.

Separately, an eraser was sold which had a two inch long metal tube for fitting the eraser on the end of any pencil. The diameter of the rubber eraser in this style of eraser was about twice the diameter of the pencil, or about one-half inch.

I have searched the internet recently, with no success, trying to locate one of these large erasers.

School desks had holes bored in the top near the top edge for a round bottle of ink. A small trench had been routed into the wood near the top edge of the desktop, a notch to hold a pencil so it would not roll off the desk which was not level on top but sloping from the front to the back near the seat.

At the high school level there were some regular desks and a few conventional armchairs with the arm intended as a writing surface and the shelf under the seat intended as the repository of books and other school equipment.

There were only eleven grades in high school in 1942 when I graduated from high school. I had only sixteen credits. The minimum required for graduation. I believe that the 12th grade was added to our Louisiana High Schools in 1947.

I was not aware until I entered Louisiana State University (LSU) in Baton Rouge that the larger high schools in the cities of the state offered many more units than were offered at Provencal, including physics, advanced algebra, foreign languages and other valuable basics. Since I was working on a science degree I had to take more courses to compensate for some of these deficiencies. My grades suffered as well.

I was playing catch up at best. I got a Bachelor of Science degree in Agricultural Economics in 1949 with an additional major in Dairy Production, 150 college credits. Later I added 26 more graduate hours in Agricultural Economics.

For those too young to remember the 1930s arrangement of the Provencal High School Grounds and building I will provide here a few notes to help you visualize it.

In 1931 the school building was a three story red brick structure. The front of the building faced to the East toward Flora. In front of the school was a large fenced in area. The fence went all the way around the school. The fence was necessary because farm animals were allowed to range freely over the countryside. The fence was built with creosoted posts and was about six feet high. The fence was made of woven wire known at the time as "hog wire" as it had been invented for the purpose of fencing hogs in or out as the need arose. So, each fenced in farm area of the community surrounding Provencal was gradually having older style fences with various heights of hog wire often and typically topped with one to three strands of barbed wire. I do not recall having seen barbed wire on the school fence.

This fence was six feet high. Some means of getting the children from the bus loading and unloading area into the school yard was necessary. This was accomplished by building a large wooden stile over the fence in two locations. One stile was in the middle of the fence in front of the school where the Hagewood-Leesville La Highway 117 road runs. Buses did not stop in that highway to discharge nor to take on students. Another stile was built over the fence on the South side of the school, a side street clearly there for the primary purpose of serving the school.

There the school buses discharged about 200 elementary students and about 120 high school students each day. The stile was a sturdy structure which began at the street level on the South side of the school fence. So when the child left the bus it was necessary to climb approximately 25 steps to get to the top of the stile. Each step went up about seven inches. There were heavy handrails built of two inch material for the small children to hold when going up or down.

At the very top of the stile was a platform about five feet wide made of two-inch lumber. The platform was about fifteen feet long. So a large number of children could stand on the top of the steps and have a good view in all directions.

There was always red mud anywhere there was any erosion in Provencal. In muddy areas of the school grounds where the trampling of many children's feet made mud holes, the school custodians filled in the holes with clinkers from the coal burning furnaces in the basement where the steam boilers providing heat to classrooms were located. This got rid of the red mud but when a child fell in the clinkers, they were as sharp as a knife and the cuts on knees and the tears in clothing were sorely dreaded by children and parents.

The entire school grounds were planted in Bermuda grass but the density of the grass most often did not protect the feet of those walking when it was wet weather. On rainy days, the student body often just did not go out of the building.

In the northeast corner of the school yard was a residence intended by the School Board to be the residence of the principal. When I was in high school from 1938 until 1942 Arthur E. Kile, principal and his wife, Dale, lived in the home with their son Coy.

Custodians at the school whom I remember were Mr. Barnes, who I recall as a pleasant light complexioned white haired elderly man who lived nearby. I recall that he had a daughter named Hazel Barnes. I believe that Mr. Ray Jackson was custodian by the time I finished school in 1942, and that Mr. Jackson had a twin sister named Faye Jackson.

School buses lined up on the south side of the school building to load or unload at the beginning and end of the school day. Most times the buses pulled in and were able to park on the side of the road near where the stile that went over the fence so children dismounting from the bus had only a short distance to go to mount the stile. This was important on rainy days and when the ground was wet or muddy. The bus drivers were expert at fairly taking turns.

Every school situation is a location where adventures take place for the young students. Provencal school certainly provided the site for one of my life's most impressive adventures. This was a venture into the public education system of the State of Louisiana.

Open Range

The establishment and development of our country provide a framework within which to understand the subsistence nature of our homestead in "No Man's Land." Land ownership and the laws associated with it evolved as the United States evolved. It is interesting to remember that The Great Depression occurred only about 150 years after the Revolutionary War and our country's subsequent independence.

Laws prior to independence proceeded from English Common Law in the thirteen colonies. Following independence, this tradition continued in a modified form. A constitution was written, a representative form of government established, and a judiciary created. English Common Law prevailed in many respects and was adapted to this new form of government. The legislative branch passed new laws that were deemed necessary and agreed with the constitution to improve the operations of the government. In principle, the laws were intended to follow what Thomas Paine would have called "Common Sense."

Basically, the laws enacted were the minimum required for the needs of the relatively sparse population of the time. They were designed to improve the functions of government. The approach and guiding principle for deciding if new legislation was necessary was embodied in the phrase "reasonable and necessary." If a law was insufficient to accomplish its goals, create a law that would improve the situation. Only if more rules were required would the legislators make the decision to enact more laws.

It is also important to remember that there were no trains, steamboats nor motorized vehicles when our government went into operation in the 1780s. Early governmental bodies met in Philadelphia and New York because Washington D. C. had not been envisioned in the beginning. The District of Columbia grew from a compromise agreement between Virginia and New York in the search for a site for the new nation's capitol city.

Horses, boats, wagons, carriages, and buggies were the primary means of traveling. It could be useful to recall that sailing was an important feature of boat transportation, but it was difficult and unreliable. Sometimes a dead calm could last for weeks. A less than favorable wind made timely the departure and arrival times impossible.

Under this evolving system of operation, the government that was initiated and grown by the Founding Fathers was not in love with taxation, arguably the reason for the fight for independence.

Observations of our laws, as the writer describes them, then includes the basics that the constitution and its primary amendments, the Bill of Rights, put into position a hundred and fifty years before the Great Depression when my memories began.

One condition of the time provided as a starting point: the ownership of real property. Real property was owned by the United States government. The U. S. Government would relinquish its ownership in numerous ways to a state, subdivision of government or an individual.

When the U. S. Government acquired any given piece of property, the property's chain of ownership was accepted. Sometimes the land contained in a state was as "purchased" by the US from Indian tribes. There were times when land was acquired from another claiming government such as Spain, France or Mexico. In the case of Texas, an independent nation-state, the occupying populace voluntarily agreed to its acquisition by the U. S. Government. This came about only one hundred years before The Great Depression. The government recognized the property ownership at the time of acquisition, sometimes acknowledging various property rights' claims such as royal land grants.

That is an area of interesting study and development. Not all political subdivisions began at the same time.

Some were a hundred years behind others. Many regions were remote from others in distance and in the time in which they came into being as political entities. So, our country had evolved to the point in 1930 that we consisted of 48 states with a flag with a star on the flag to represent each of those 48 states.

As you can see, land ownership did not come about in any single manner. There were many ways claims came about and many ways acquisitions were made throughout history. So now consider Thomas Jefferson's 1803 purchase of a huge expanse of land from France, the transaction famously known as The Louisiana Purchase. This acquisition happened within this rather loose arrangement of land ownership. The United States Government discovered many residual territorial claim disputes between the two most recent owners of Louisiana, France and Spain. Since France no longer was a party to the disputes, the USA acquired the land and the incumbent disputes with Spain.

In 1803, Spain had a major claim pertinent to the area of Natchitoches Parish. Spain claimed ownership of all land west of the Red River in the region. The United States claimed that the purchase of Louisiana included all the land westward from the Red River to the Sabine River, the latter being the modern border between the states of Louisiana and Texas.

Spain and the fledgling United States wanted to avoid fighting by seeking a temporary compromise. The governments negotiated a land ownership agreement that included the following: neither country would establish any government forts nor enforce laws in the disputed region. The disputed region in this agreement was between the Rio Hondo, a small stream about six miles west of Natchitoches running Southward, and the Sabine River. Hence, that area between the two streams became known as "No Man's Land." This "No Man's Land" was roughly 50 miles wide and 200 miles long.

At that time Natchitoches Parish constituted all of northwest Louisiana.

Outlaws from any direction were drawn to the region when being pursued by any government for law violation. There was no law there to control them and no government with authority to authorize neither extradition nor pursuit into the territory.

I perceive that this situation provided a basis for development of independent, self-reliant characters on the part of those who lived there, who relied on their own ability to control their destinies, including conduct, self-defense and ownership of land and other property, particularly livestock. Perhaps there could have been the origin of the saying, "Him that gets there firstest with the mostest controls," a kind of law of the land as understood by occupants of government land on the frontier, particularly in the early west and possibly even more particularly in "No Man's Land."

By the 1930s the territorial dispute over "No Man's Land" had long been settled. When Texas gained independence from Mexico the land dispute became moot. The United States controlled all land to the Sabine River and that part became Louisiana. Texas was across the Sabine River and had become part of the USA as well.

All of this state of affairs in 1860 when the War Between the States began, was ripe for solving some land ownership questions, but would have to wait until after the Civil War. Soon after the surrender of Robert E. Lee, the United States needed to repay those who had been loyal and fought for the Union. The government also needed to repay those from whom the government had borrowed money with which to fight the war. In order to meet that need, partially and additionally in order to encourage the populating of newly acquired areas westward, the Homestead Act was passed and local land ownership began to change. Citizens who patented claims in No Man's Land could become owners of limited amounts of land by meeting provisions of the Act. Our homestead near Provencal had been one of the properties homesteaded earlier. For this reason such properties were often referred to by their new owners as "the homestead" even though they were not the original person to homestead the land legally.

Surrounding such plots of land in the sand hills of the Kisatchie region were huge tracts of land that were sold to investors by the United States government around the 1890s, about 25 to 30 years after the end of the Civil War. All land in the 1930s which was not fenced in the Kisatchie Hills, and for the most part all of the piney woods of parishes of Louisiana, was called "Open Range."

"Open Range" meant that anyone who wished could allow livestock they owned to range freely and forage over any land not fenced in by the owner.

In the 130 years since the Revolutionary War, a Federal Government was established with an amendable constitution using adaptations of English Common Law and given the ability to acquire land for the nation's expansion. This is the framework within which property ownership and rights existed. A land dispute between nations, a Civil War, and a growth in population determined much of the laws that led to the "Open Range."

This set of laws permitted something germane to the very survival of subsistence farmers of the region during the Great Depression. Without the privilege of allowing our cattle, hogs, goats and sheep to range freely and graze on all the land we would have faced near starvation. Sometimes we faced it in spite of the open range. The unfenced land was owned by large land owners, mostly lumber companies, who had harvested all the turpentine and lumber from the virgin pine forests of the region between about 1895 and 1925.

Due to these prevailing laws and practices, John D. owned about twenty head of cattle, enough to provide all the milk needed by the resident members of the family, typically about ten persons during the depression years. Further he owned about a half dozen brood sows which ranged freely on the range near our homestead. They, unlike the feral hogs on these lands today, were fairly well domesticated, fed enough regularly to keep them somewhat tame and under the control of the owner of the brand or ear mark. John D. also owned up to one hundred goats.

From these animals came milk, butter, beef, pork, and kid meat plus small amounts of home needs acquired by barter or sale of animals and their products. There were occasional sales for cash, but the shortage of money made this the exception.

Residents of the region who had the resources extended themselves into the livestock enterprises on their homestead. The extent to which they did so was in ratio to needs, health and ability of family members to care for the animals and their management ability.

During the Great Depression the open range arrangement operated well because each livestock owner had horses which were a virtual necessity in managing range cattle and hogs. They went along together. The subsistence farmer grew corn to feed his team and riding animals. Part of the corn was used to fatten the hogs that were kept on the open range. The same corn field produced the corn which was to be ground at a local grist mill, such as Henry McGaskey's near the Sylvest homestead. From the same corn supply came the chicken feed to produce poultry and eggs for consumption and barter.

Parallel to the crop enterprise, corn, was growing of hay. The hay met the needs of the riding animals, work team and the milking herd.

Access to the open range as a source of free pasture was an essential element in the equation that resulted in survival.

A major change took place in the 1930s and 1940s when gasoline-powered automobiles and trucks along with the building and paving altered the prevailing life styles. A person no longer had to be able to walk to his work site nor live next to it as on the horse powered subsistence farm of 1930.

Shortly, as the years went by, the open range was not the integral object which enabled survival under conditions of high unemployment and shortage of money and credit. After The Great Depression, mobility was paramount; the family car and pickup truck became the integral object for survival.

A visit to the region in 2013 by the author reminded him of this substantial change in dependence and independence. Many of the occupants of pieces of property in the Kisatchie National Forest near my birthplace live in a home built on a former family homestead, but the occupant is employed up to a hundred miles away in a city or even in another state.

Along with this mobility came the flexibility of moving great distances quickly by automobile. Car pools were an early invention of the farm boys around Provencal who were no longer imprisoned by how far they could ride a horse to work daily. He could ride in a truck with three neighbors and work in a refinery in Beaumont and come home to see his girlfriend or wife and children at the end of his shift.

Time does change things.

These same occupants of the old homesteads became college graduates, taught school, commuted to

Shreveport to work for a telephone company, and hung on to local family values while at the same time becoming affluent enough to become hunting club members whose organizations now lease the timber company land which was grandpa's open range.

Times do change.

Medicine and Health Care

To consider the conditions of the time requires some background information, often called assumptions in writings of many kinds.

Medicine or a doctor could not be accessed on short notice, because of limited communications, and transportation. Remember, no telephones and no motorized vehicle at more than 95 percent of the surrounding homesteads and no improved roads except for main routes could accommodate a motorized vehicle, if one were available.

The exposure of the entire family to health risks was never far from the minds of these remotely located settlers. Living on subsistence farms in the piney woods of Natchitoches Parish was accompanied by many hazards. Potential accidents were numerous. One could be bit by animals both domestic and wild. Falls from horseback or horse-drawn vehicles were not unusual. Bodily injuries from accidents with any animal-drawn farm implement. Trees fell on sawyers. One may fall from trees which often had to be climbed for various reasons including harvesting of fruit, both home grown and in the wild. These are only a few of the ways one could be injured.

Beyond accidents and bodily injuries were the many diseases that were common: measles, mumps, scarlet fever, typhoid fever, croup, ear infections, tuberculosis, chicken pox, and pneumonia. Internal ailments were discussed by my parents because certain neighbors had cancer, others had stomach ulcers, and some had diabetes as did my mother.

Our homestead possessed better knowledge of health maintenance than the usual piney woods farm. That, because Minnie Fendlason Sylvest was the granddaughter of Doctor David Harrison Stringfield, M D who graduated from Tulane University in 1860. While the level of study and scientific knowledge was far inferior to what it was when I graduated from high school in 1942 at the beginning of World War II, common means to stop bleeding, set simple fractures and medicate open wounds were known.

John D. Sylvest was regarded as knowledgeable as the local community general practitioners in treating pneumonia in the 1930s, before antibiotics. I came to know this of my father because the doctor who delivered me in 1925, Dr. Addison, said as much. In 1936 one of our neighbors asked Dr. Addison what was being done for their teen age daughter with pneumonia. They wanted him to come see and treat her. The doctor, when told that Mr. Sylvest was assisting in treating her, was quoted as having said, "Just do what Mr. Sylvest tells you. He knows as much about treating pneumonia as I do."

There is no claim to fame in admitting the limited knowledge level that existed at the time. Sulfa drugs had not come into local use in the early 1930s. Penicillin was not to come into use until well into the 1940s.

This is from my own observations and experience, not history and medical research records.

The pneumonia victim being treated as described above was hospitalized in Natchitoches but did not survive.

I had pneumonia myself in 1944 and was treated with sulfa drugs when I was in basic training in World War II. I remained in the hospital two weeks being treated for the pneumonia.

I saw actual 1 X 4 inch boards trimmed down with a hatchet, hand saw and carving knife used as splints on people who had broken forearms. Maybe there were some plaster of Paris casts in the piney woods during the 1930s but I do not remember seeing but a few during my school years, 1931 to 1942.

The medicine cabinet contained Aspirin in tablet form. Pepsin, an enzyme extracted from baby pigs, I was told, was kept in syrup form to give to children who had digestive troubles. I took the medicine within my memory. I cannot attest to my age at the time.

For wounds such as axe cuts we applied a generous amount of "ichthyol" salve, such as half an ounce, and bandaged it tightly so the wound would be held together in such a position that it would discourage bleeding plus grow back together and heal. Stitches were not common on many minor and some major wounds within my experience. If such were required the subject often was relocated from the site of the accident to a hospital in Natchitoches, Alexandria or Shreveport.

I almost cut off the toe next to my great toe on my left foot with an axe when I was splitting kindling at age 14. Blood went everywhere. My mother and father quickly wrapped the wound with a piece of towel to slow the bleeding. They had me lie on my back and keep my left foot elevated in the air to retard the bleeding. When the bleeding had slowed enough, they put the salve on the wound and wrapped it in strips of cloth torn from a discarded muslin bed sheet. This bandage was to hold the flesh of the toe in position. The bone was not broken but the flesh of the toe was cut more than fifty percent of the way around the bone. The wound healed, after the required time for healing, a few weeks. I was able to go to school while disabled.

Ruth and I were playing some kind of spin around game in our living room when I slung her someway and she fell and hit her head on the edge of the piano cutting it to the skull and possibly fracturing the skull. Again, the salve and heavy wrapping of an old sheet torn into strips was used and Ruth was kept still for a period of time until healing took place.

My friend and neighbor, Raymond Kay, at age about 13, around 1938 was thrown from his family wagon. A mule ran off the road and the wagon turned over. The mule had been frightened by a canvas flapping on a (Civilian Conservation Corps) CCC truck passing the wagon on the gravel road now known as LA Highway 117. The truck stopped and the CCC men took Raymond to the CCC camp medical doctor at the camp just below Bellwood, LA on LA 117. The bones of the arm were set and immobilized by what I think may have been wood splints. Rapid healing took place. Before he finished high school Raymond became a creditable baseball pitcher for Provencal High School.

That big man could flat throw a baseball.

Laxatives were kept such as Cascara pills, and a commercial mixture called Black Draught. A tonic called 666 or "Three Sixes" was in most medicine cabinets.

Epsom Salts were used as a laxative sometimes and was kept on hand on the Sylvest homestead should there be a need for internal or for topical uses. Soaking an infection on a foot in an Epsom salts bath was a frequent treatment.

Internal parasites were not unknown in the piney woods. Round worms were identified sometimes by the State Board of Health physician. Hook worms were not unknown and were identified in the same way and treated.

When I was in high school, the Natchitoches Parish doctor serving with the State Board of Health was Dr. Knipmeyer. Periodically this doctor and his nurse and staff visited all the schools in the parish beginning sometime in the late 1930s. Such services from the State and Parish increased in frequency from the time I started school in 1931 until I graduated in 1942.

One of my mother's favorites was Castor Oil. It is an evil tasting liquid and was, until a few decades ago, still used by the medical professions as a purgative. It was given to completely empty the digestive tract. Of that, it was supremely capable. Castor Oil must be a vicious poison that the body detests. I recall the very mention of the word caused me to have a nauseous feeling. I must have been about 14 when Minnie insisted that I take a dose of Castor Oil. I resisted every way I could without being violent. I begged my mother not to force me to take it. She eventually relented enough to promise me that if I took the dose she had in mind for me she would never require nor force me to take Castor Oil again. I was not dumb. Minnie's promise was "money in the bank." I jumped at the chance. Took the medicine and she never asked me to take Castor Oil again.

Minor surgeries were included in the necessary treatments performed at home. If an infection needed to be opened so it could drain, call on Minnie. She would scrub the offending area well with soap and water, then, in later years, sterilize it further with denatured alcohol. She would then heat the sewing needle over the top of the chimney of a kerosene lamp flame. With that you had a sterile weapon with which to pick an opening in a boil, a common problem resulting from staph infections on the farm.

Often a splinter from a piece of wood would stab the hand or foot and break off in the flesh. Sometimes this sliver of wood would penetrate so deep that it, or parts of it, could not be located easily. A small, hand-held magnifying glass was one of the pieces of equipment in our first-aid supplies. (I think it resided with my father's bible most of the time to be used as a reading glass.) Sometimes the offending foreign material would be so well imbedded that it could not be seen and dug out with the razor blade or knife blade used as the surgical instrument. Oh! Yes!

A sharp pocket knife was kept by adult male residents of the piney woods not only to use on farm animals for ear marking and castrating, but for use on human patients in need of minor surgeries as well. Modern doctors shudder at the thought of such treatments and remedies. So, do I.

I can recall a wood splinter imbedded in my finger. The home appointed surgeon could not locate the offender. I remember John D. saying that it was not a large, dangerous splinter. Although it would be painful until it was removed, he suggested it would be best to make a salt meat patch and bandage. This treatment was intended to soften the flesh and make removing the splinter easier. And so, a wrapping of a slice of salted cured pork was applied under a bandage and over the foreign object. Within a few days the area of discomfort and pain was localized. When the bandage was removed, the needle procedure revealed the splinter's location and facilitated its removal. The wound needed draining and then it was scrubbed and medicated. More washing with soapy water was required and more sterilizing the area with denatured alcohol followed. The ever present "Ichthyol" (Trade name probably) salve was applied to prevent further infection during the healing process. It has occurred to me that Mother Nature included in her package an system of infection with the associated festering which surrounded the foreign object with the dead white blood cells we called "pus." This pus loosened the foreign object and enabled it to exit the opening in the skin through which it had entered the flesh in the first place. I recall a festering taking place about two days after a splinter being imbedded in the flesh of my finger. The splinter at this point was easy to remove as a bit of pressure on the wound caused it to slide out through the original path of entry. The pain relief occurred immediately upon the release of the pressure in the festered wound and the exit of the offending foreign body.

Not to be found as a proposed chapter in modern medical textbooks as standard medical and surgical procedure, this set of actions under the constant experienced supervision of parents met the needs of many everyday emergencies in the piney woods of the 1930s when getting a patient to a doctor could take several days. Most frequently, searching for a doctor was skipped even as a possible option.

I remember Minnie washing and boiling a white muslin bed sheet to sterilize it for use as bandaging material. It was torn into strips of various widths so a suitable size could be selected to match the needs of the size and location of the wound.

Looking back on the education levels of parents of the time, most parents just followed the habits of sanitation at the level taught them by their own parents. Sometimes, for certain households of friends I visited the practices were woefully short of those I observed as taught by Minnie and John D. Minnie had completed high school and John D. eventually took a test and got a GED, I have been told by elder siblings.

My parents were often called upon by neighbors as consultants on certain procedure such as attending to wounds much as they were consulted on a variety of other homestead activities such as making cane syrup, butchering farm animals, curing all kinds of meat produced on the farm, and canning all kinds of fruit and vegetables.

Though we drank raw milk, they were aware of the pasteurization process and the temperatures called for in sterilizing food or utensils. Our very successful canning operation that continued year after year with rare spoilage attested to that.

I provide this observation from a somewhat informed perspective because I later majored in Dairy Science and studied Chemistry and Microbiology as part of my curriculum.

I recall that in high school chemistry class in 1942 I was told by Horace Hays, Chemistry and Science teacher at Provencal High School, that the number of known chemical compounds was doubling every year and that could be a good field to study at college.

Mr. Hays, later became "Dr. Hays," retired as a professor from Kansas State University. Hays married Thelma Beasley, my English teacher. I went to school with Thelma's brothers, Prentiss and Clifton Beasley both tall stalwarts on the Provencal High School basketball team.

The Town of Provencal

The town of Provencal, when I started to school in 1931, consisted of a settlement of 800 persons, according to the 1930 U. S. Census. The town had no official limits as far as I know. The population was spread over an area about one to two miles in diameter as I estimate it to have been.

You may refer to the Photos and Map section of this book to see the related maps.

The Texas and Pacific Railroad ran east and west through Provencal on a rail roadway that began in Addis, LA in West Baton Rouge or Iberville Parish just west of Baton Rouge and ran to Shreveport. Louisiana

State Highway 39 (currently numbered 117) ran north and south as an improved gravel road from Hagewood (otherwise sometimes known as Coldwater) to Leesville about 50 miles.

Provencal Creek, shown as Provencal Bayou on some maps, runs from west to east through the south edge of Provencal, officially a village of about 1100 inhabitants as of the 2000 US census.

The landmark structures which were in position in the 1930s included Provencal High School, a three-story, red brick structure which was located near the present school site.

From the vantage point of the second and third floors of the three-story school building could be seen many of the activities of the town. The school was near the northern edge of the thickly populated area as it continues to be in 2013.

The train depot was on the south side of the railroad which, for convenience in describing the locations of things and actions nearby, we can call the "tracks." The depot was west of the graveled highway which we can just call, "LA 117," as it is now designated.

The train tracks passed only about two or three blocks south of the school.

The passenger train passed through Provencal about 9:15 am daily on its way to Shreveport. At that time of day the school buses had arrived in town and school children were in class. From the classrooms on the south side of the school, the students could hear the whistle of the locomotive as it approached Provencal from the direction of Flora. There was a standard pattern to the blowing of the whistle, a certain number of short and long blasts of the steam whistle to indicate where the train was located and what the engineer operating the engine intended to do. The whistle we heard from school told us daily that the coal burning steam engine was approaching with about four cars attached. Along with the whistle, there was the ringing of the bell on the engine as it approached the depot.

The first car in line behind the engine was the coal car which was there for the purpose of providing the coal to be burned constantly while the engine was running and pulling the train that day. Water and coal stops were regular as required. I do not remember seeing the train being serviced. A phenomenon not now observed was boxcars loaded with coal. Provencal High School was the only building in town which consumed coal as fuel.

The next car in line behind the coal car was the baggage car. The baggage car was the location of mail and packages including the trunks and luggage of passengers on the train. Following the baggage car there were usually two passenger cars.

As you may expect, I must call your attention more forcibly to the fact that, as the engine burned coal, there was an abundance of cinders and black smut which kept being blown out of the smokestack. As the engine pulled the railcars rather than pushing them, the cars followed the engine which led the way. Hence, whatever the smokestack dispensed was available to fly into the open windows of the passenger cars except during the winter when the passenger car windows were closed. Closing the windows only partially protected passengers from the coal dust and smoke. Sometimes a small cinder would burn a pin hole in your dress shirt or dress.

There was no air-conditioning for comfort or for cleanliness. Nor was there an effective heating system.

The first desire of dismounting passengers, of which there were few in Provencal, was to access the washing facilities wherever they were.

Each morning stop required only about five minutes to discharge all passengers, baggage and mail at the depot. In those minutes, the school children on the south side of the school could hear the daily hustle and bustle of loading and unloading passengers, mail and luggage. The whistle of the train and ringing of the bell as the engineer announced that the train was going to move forward could be heard by all occupants of the school.

The huffing and puffing of the straining engine as it struggled to get the heavy train in motion again could be heard on takeoff. Within two or three minutes those students near open windows could hear the characteristic whistle sound as the train disappeared west and north toward Victoria, Robeline, Marthaville, Pleasant Hill, Mansfield and the other smaller stops along the entire way to Shreveport.

The train returned on its way from Shreveport back to Alexandria in the afternoon, reaching Provencal near 2:30 pm. As I recall, it passed the school on the evening return trip before the school buses departed from the school. As school schedules are somewhat flexible due to weather, sporting events, and such, there were school days when the time the school buses were departing at the end of the school day, about 3:00 pm, was about the time the train could be expected to go through Provencal.

I make this observation because there was abject fear of any driver ever colliding with a train, particularly the driver of a school bus. A characteristic of a train that we feared most was the distance required for a train to stop.

The use of the train by passengers gradually declined from the 1920s into the 1930s. I observed this decline in the 1940s before graduating high school. The passenger train was still a useful means of transportation to Provencal and surrounding communities. I used it to go to Alexandria numerous times when I was enroute from Provencal to Baton Rouge in the late 1940s. Provencal had no bus line serving the town in the 1930s and 1940s, the closest being in Natchitoches. One route we took to get from Provencal to Baton Rouge was taking the train in Provencal to Alexandria. We would then transfer from the train to the Greyhound Bus lines in Alexandria.

The T & P train from Provencal did not go to Baton Rouge on the east side of the Mississippi River. It went to Addis, LA on the west side. In addition, there was not a direct train route from Addis to Baton Rouge nor was there a convenient bus connecting Addis and Baton Rouge, as they are on opposite sides of the Mississippi River.

Over the period from the 1920s to the 1940s, there was a gradual increase in the number of automobiles in use in Provencal as in the whole country. As the number of vehicles increased, more miles of roads were improved and additional routes developed.

This entire change was so gradual that at the time I hardly realized it was happening. Looking back at it in 2013 it is totally unbelievable as having happened during a single lifetime.

The entire nation transitioned from horses and wagons combined with steam-powered trains just after 1900 into a nation of internal combustion powered automobiles, trucks, trains and airplanes in the 1950s, a fairly brief period of about five decades. During that time two major world wars were fought, World War I in Europe from 1914 to 1918, followed by World War II from 1935 until 1945. The United States entered WW I in 1917 and WW II in 1941.

So, in the 1930s and 1940s the railroad was still a significant method of transportation from Provencal to Shreveport, and Alexandria, Louisiana and points north and south of Provencal.

The school children in Provencal daily witnessed the passenger train going north and west in the morning and returning east and south in the afternoon.

The Texas and Pacific rails through Provencal were accompanied by one or two side tracks which paralleled the main line for a half mile or so as a side track. The side track was not immediately adjacent to the main track at all points. It angled off to a distance of about 200 feet to allow for loading and unloading of freight.

From 1930 until 1942 I could hear the sounds of loading on the side track. Logs, poles, and piling were loaded on boxcars positioned on this side track.

Cross ties, the nine-foot long timbers hewed by hand from trees destined for building and repairing the foundations of the rails, were noisily loaded by hand. Wagons pulled by horses and mules hauled most of the ties from 1930 until about 1935. Then, flatbed trucks with specially built bodies to haul cross ties gradually replaced the teams and wagons from about 1935 until about 1940. By 1942, when I graduated from Provencal High School, no cross ties were delivered to the railroad by horse and mule teams. Trucks took over those jobs.

In fact, during the decade of the 1930s, trucks replaced horse and mule teams as the means of hauling timber and timber products. As time passed, trucks also replaced the railroads for hauling all timber products.

After about 1942 there was no longer to be heard, forever, the mule skinner's voice yelling, "Whoa!" to stop his team. Also, no longer would be heard the booms of the piling as it tumbled into the boxcar just off the school grounds.

Luther Thibodeaux is the last of the Provencal teamsters I remember loading timber into boxcars on the Provencal side track. I went to school with Mr. Luther's children. One of his sons, Garland, was only a few years older than I.

I think the side track location was near the depot. South of the depot was a store owned by Ralph Osborne and purchased about 1939 by Westbrook.

On the corner next to Osborne's Store was a store owned by Monroe Hawthorne. Mrs. Hazel Hawthorne, his wife, taught me in the second grade in 1932.

South of Mr. Monroe's store was a store and filling station owned by Myles Key and his wife, Evergreen. They had a son named Luther Key who was a devastating marksman with a 22 caliber rifle.

On the south side of the Key store was the Provencal Post Office. The Postmaster when I was in school was Mr. John Voight. Mr. Voight had a son named Johnny Voight, who had a sons named Buck and Max, who were in school with me.

Continuing south through Provencal on the west side of the highway, that doubled as the main street, after passing the post office, the road made a 90-degree turn to the left, heading east before turning south again after only one block. Immediately after the turn on the right, was the Tom Key garage and filling station, the southernmost business place in Provencal in 1942.

About a half block from Mr. Key's garage on the same side of the street was the Methodist church.

Across the highway from the post office was the largest general merchandise store in the town, Harry Hawthorne's

Store. Many times when in elementary school I took a dozen eggs in a half gallon syrup can to the Hawthorne store to exchange for a pound of coffee. After the exchange was transacted, Mrs. Nan Hawthorne, Mr. Harry's wife, would sometimes slip me a penny stick of peppermint candy. The stick of candy helped relieve the pain of having to sacrifice my recess play time to make the trip to the store from school to take care of the eggs for coffee transaction.

Recently I learned that in later years the Hawthorne store was owned and operated by my classmate, A. J. Scarborough and, I believe, his brother, another friend of mine, J. B. Scarborough. My teacher in the fourth grade in 1934 was Magdalene Scarborough who became the wife of Mr. Harry Hawthorne's son, Lynn Hawthorne, later a professor at Louisiana State University. I do not know if Magdalene was related to A. J. and J. B.

Across the highway from the school was what I remember being called the Apostolic Church. I recall a minister who pastored the church named Haley. Reverend Haley had several children with whom I attended school; Howard, Hersel and Reba were three. Later Hersel married my classmate, Beatrice Moss, daughter of Luther and Amanda Moss.

The third church in Provencal that I remember was the Baptist church located where it is today just west of Provencal school.

Immediately across the highway from the school was a brick residence owned by Mr. "Red" Milam. I never learned his real name. Mr. Milam had a daughter named Veonia who was a classmate of mine. As I recall, Marcelle Dowden was valedictorian of our class and Veonia was Salutatorian. Congratulations, Veonia, wherever you are. Mr. Milam was a distributor of Mobil Oil petroleum products and owned a filling station and garage across from the school near the "Y" intersection.

A convenience store/gas station/restaurant now occupies the spot. I believe it is the only place in Provencal where gasoline is for sale in 2013.

Soil Conservation

Agriculture in the 1930s, as described throughout this series of essays covers the practices of the time. Interesting things were taking place politically as Franklin D. Roosevelt replaced Herbert Hoover as President of the United States in 1932 when I was seven years old. The Roosevelt Administration turned its attention to many things in the troubled nation including agriculture.

Numerous federal agencies relating to agriculture were formed as extensions of the Executive Branch of government. They operated under the United States Department of Agriculture (USDA). Some of these were the Agricultural Adjustment Act (AAA), The Farmer's

Home Administration (FHA), the Soil Conservation Service (SCS), and the Farm Credit Administration (FCA), to name a few.

A major problem in the hill country was soil erosion. When the virgin timber was cut from the hillsides of the South, including all the rolling, hilly land of Kisatchie National Forest, the roots of the vegetation were no longer there to hold the soil in position. As a result, fast flowing water pouring down sandy hillsides washed out huge amounts of sandy soil leaving gullies of all sizes, some large enough to hold houses.

The Soil Conservation Service, in particular, and some other agencies were assigned to educate and assist the farmers of the hill country throughout the South in the technique of contour plowing to control erosion. One of the problems encountered by the SCS was that there were not enough engineers and surveyors with the equipment to run the lines of the contours in the fields of the farms simultaneously. So, the program continued for years.

John D. would address that problem himself. As an experienced builder and contractor, he knew about elevations and how to keep buildings level. With no transit available, he would just improvise. From the days of the pioneers, settlers, particularly farmers, had become ingenuous at improvising as they populated the whole United States. Those who became good at it could solve problems and contribute to their prosperity. John D. was good at it.

Taking his ten-year old son into his blacksmith shop as an assistant, John D. took out his carpentry tool box containing a carpenter's level, about 36 inches long. With several planed one-inch by four-inch pieces of lumber, a framing square, a tri-square, a carpenter's pencil and a hand saw, of the "cut-off" variety, i. e., 10 points(teeth) per inch, he laid out and cut boards for an "A" frame. The wood frame was about seven feet tall at the apex of the frame. The cross timber which completed the alphabetic shaped frame of a capital "A" was about five feet from the ground. That height was selected because as the resting place of the carpenter's level, it needed to be at approximately the height of a man's eye when he was standing. The legs of the frame were about twelve feet apart.

With this substitute for a surveyor's scope and a boy to precede him across the field with a stick to sight upon his instructions, John D. laid out the lines around the hillsides of Sylvest farm.

Beginning at the highest point in the field, John D. directed me in a line which was level around the hill. I proceeded to drive stakes where instructed. After running the first line near the crown of the hill, John D. moved down the hillside and determined another line about three feet lower than the first line. Each line was then followed with a plow and additional rows were plowed about thirty-six inches apart in between these master lines. The master rows, which were to become terraces, to retard the flow of run-off rainwater were laid out. If the slope was gentle, the terraces could be a long distance apart, even up to a hundred feet if the slope was nearly flat or level. If the slope of the fields was steep, the terraces would be closer together.

Earthen terraces with a width at their base of about fifteen feet were laid out in all fields on the farm. The terraces, about two feet high in the center were constructed with a turning plow and a homemade, horse-drawn grader. As the soil was graded up into a mound two feet high and fifteen feet wide, drainage of water was directed by the terraces horizontally. This retarded the flow of the water so the soil was not washed away by rushing water taking the shortest route down the hill and carrying much sandy soil with it.

It took all winter to lay out and build the terraces, with rows in between, at the proper elevations, and to grade the terraces into a strong form. While the fields had had rows purporting to be approximately level before, the surveying that was done refined the layout with improved precision.

About 1938, a representative of the Soil Conservation Service came to Sylvest farm to layout the terraces. They checked all the terraces and found that the accuracy with which they were laid out was such that none of the terraces had to be relocated. That "A" frame and a carpenter's level with John D. behind the wheel to drive and a boy to carry a stick and drive stakes had met the demands at the beginning of the rush to the technological age about 1938, in the middle of the Great Depression.

Can't afford an engineer with a transit to survey your terraces, just improvise; figure out a way to do it yourself.

Terraces in the fields required management and maintenance. One specific practice which aided the effort was the planting of crops on the terraces which would produce roots which in turn helped to hold the soil in place. Sometimes the crop would just be whatever crop was being grown on the adjacent contoured rows. Other times we planted specialty crops on the terraces such as watermelons or peanuts.

Early after the development of the terraced fields, we discovered that the terraces were supremely adapted to the growing of watermelons which require a large area because the plants grow vines as long as thirty feet from the base of the plant. The root systems which grew and sustained such large stems and long vines were likewise extensive. Growing our watermelon crop on the terraced rows became our regular practice.

John D. and Minnie had brought seeds of watermelons from Washington Parish to Pineville, La in 1916 and then to Provencal when they moved there in 1923. It was a special novelty variety known and appreciated for its extra sweetness. It was called "Heavenly Melons" not because they tasted so good, which they did, but because each melon had a solid green color which was spotted with bright yellow spots. Typically a melon had one large yellow spot up to three inches in diameter plus up to fifty smaller yellow spots. These spots were described as "the moon and the stars" thus providing the foundation for the name of the variety of watermelons. Sylvest farm watermelons were well known in the community because of their sweetness and because of their color. Some of our melons weighed as much as fifty pounds.

Seeds and Plant Propagation

The subsistence mode of living in the sand hills during the Great Depression included the survival practice of growing absolutely everything we needed to survive if we could do so. Growing any single item, whether ornamental, vegetable or crop, for human consumption, livestock feed or market required consideration of the propagation process for those plants. For most plants that meant growing, harvesting and preserving the seed from year to year.

For a few crops, it meant managing the propagation and preservation of the plant species by some form of vegetative process, meaning saving appropriate plant parts from one growing season until the next.

A few crops did not lend themselves well to either of these homespun processes. Special arrangements were sometimes made to purchase the seed such as Austrian Winter peas and common vetch, which we grew as winter cover crops. Both of these crops were of nitrogen fixing character, legumes, so they helped fertilize the soil both as the organic cover crop when plowed under and as the nitrogen fixing crop. We did not have the equipment required to save the seed of the peas and vetch. It was difficult to acquire the cash with which to purchase those two kinds of seed. The inoculation material for the peas had to be purchased as we had no means of producing it. That meant another cash purchase.

Seed Propagated Plants

For most crops, including cotton and corn, the standard procedure was selecting the plants from which seed were to be saved, harvesting the plants, capturing the desired seed and preserving them until the following year. This was done to many vegetable garden plants as well.

Other crops for which we saved seed were peanuts and velvet beans.

Peanuts were grown for human consumption and as a feed crop for livestock. The vines were used as hay for cows and mules and horses after the peanuts were removed by hand. Some of the peanuts were preserved as seed. The seed of the peanut itself grows on an underground stem.

Velvet beans were grown on land concurrently with corn. Appropriate amounts of the velvet beans were harvested by hand as soon as they were mature and dry enough. These were kept as seed for the next year. Two benefits came from growing the velvet beans. The plant on which the beans grew was a legume so it had some nitrogen fixing characteristics. It also had some value as forage, though most of the leaves fell off by the time the bean pods were dry. The beans were highly nutritious as cattle feed so we practiced allowing the cattle to graze in the cornfields after we had harvested the corn. By using this scheme we avoided the hand labor of picking the beans. Hogs were also allowed to forage for the waste corn and beans in the field after the cattle had been removed.

Preserving cottonseed from year to year meant retrieving the seed from the gin after the lint cotton had been removed by ginning. Lint was sold separately. We produced more seed than the amount required to plant our cotton acreage the following year, so some of the cottonseed were traded for cottonseed meal which was good to plow under as a nitrogen rich fertilizer the following spring. Otherwise the cottonseed meal was a valuable cattle feed. We did both, depending upon the need.

While this memoir is not a scientific horticultural treatise, it could be interesting to some readers to learn what hand-operated exercises we went through in harvesting, processing and preserving the various seeds each year on the Sylvest homestead.

Vegetable Seed

It was the common practice to save two or three times as much seed as would be needed for the next year in the event pests such as insects, rodents or farm animals destroyed any of our seed supply. Although special precautions were taken to avoid such disasters, sometimes they occurred.

To keep the weevils out, our seed were mixed with generous amounts of an insect powder sold at the time under the trade name of "Bee Brand Insect Powder." It was filled with organic ingredients which repulsed insects. I do not know those ingredients.

Root crops including turnips, mustard, radishes, beets and carrots were grown but seed for them were usually ordered from Hastings or Reuter Seeds. Sometimes we bought them at the local general merchandise stores in Provencal. If not available in Provencal, Natchitoches was sometimes the closest source.

Frequently, we got some seed from a neighbor who had more than enough to share. A few species were especially interesting such as the "Heavenly" watermelons.

Okra was of special interest because we grew one large disease resistant variety to insure an abundance should our other varieties fail. It was called cow horn okra and produced a stalk that sometimes grew sixteen feet tall. With stalks that tall it was a challenge to bend the stalk over and gather the harvestable pods of okra without breaking the tall stalk or uprooting the plant. With care, each stalk would produce okra for several weeks in the summer and fall seasons. The individual pods of okra were sometimes over twelve inches in length. Sometimes the individual pods were almost an inch in diameter. We usually had an ample supply to share with neighbors who had none. We also habitually saved large amounts of seed for planting and sharing. Seed sharing was just an ongoing practice that characterized the geographical region, the hills of the Southern states.

An interesting characteristic of the okra plant is that it can cause severe itching resulting from contact with the plant by the bare skin during the harvesting process. As a consequence of this, severe discomfort would often occur and continue for hours. Certain individuals are more susceptible to this allergic reaction than others. My mother tolerated the okra itch very well. However, she put on gloves and/or covered her hands and arms with something such as old sleeves removed from an old shirt. This kept her hands and arms from contacting the plant.

In the late 1930s a new variety called velvet okra came on the market. The billing on the new variety indicated that it would not cause you to itch. It was much better than the cow horn okra as far as causing the harvester to itch. It still caused certain people to itch severely.

If one could tolerate the itching caused by the cow horn variety, it was a far more productive variety. Many bushels of okra could be picked from a couple of 200 foot rows of cow horn okra in one growing season.

My sister, Ruth, still has some of the seed to this variety of okra which was handed down to our family by my grandmother, Lillian Stringfield Fendlason.

Another special vegetable was the spotted butter bean. The climbing variety was the favorite. The dried mature bean seeds were spotted and were so colorful with shades of purple and pink that they make a beautiful display on a table or window sill when kept in view in a transparent glass fruit jar. There is such a jar of those seed on display in the house in which I reside. I have lived in that house continuously since I had it built in 1968. Those beans in that jar were given to me by my sister, Ruth, who told me she had grown them from beans handed down from the garden of my maternal grandmother, Lillian Stringfield Fendlason who grew them in Washington Parish and gave some seed to our mother, Minnie.

The Chris Reuter Seed Company was founded in 1929. H. G. Hastings published a seed catalog as well. These two mail order seed sources contributed substantially to survival of the population in the rural South during The Great Depression.

I recall two instances related to seed from the 1930s. They still entertain me. Reuter sent a representative out into the countryside before roads were improved in the 1930s searching for seed of as many varieties of vegetables and flowers as they could obtain from anyone. Keeping in mind that when one looks at the seed of a vegetable, the person cannot know what plant and flower the seed will produce. I remember my mother sharing seed and information about the seed with the Reuter Seed Company representative around 1938. I remember my mother, Minnie Sylvest and John D. discussing the Reuter Seed Company and its search for any seed variety whatsoever so it could propagate and sell the seed. That was an invaluable service to the rural population of the South as growing our food was our primary means of survival. Thank you, Chris Reuter, a benefactor long deceased.

The other instance I recall about seed, as we knew them during the 1930s, is the other seed catalog from H. G. Hastings. There was a variety of corn which we grew on the Sylvest homestead called Hastings Prolific. I believe it is and was available from Pioneer Seed Company. Around 1935 John D. decided he would like to grow the yellow corn rather than the white as the yellow corn kernel is just a bit softer than the white. This feature of softer kernels was considered desirable as livestock eating corn wore their teeth out prematurely due to the hard kernels of the white corn plus the contamination with sand, from the sandy soil on which the crops grew.

I do not recall that the popularity of the yellow dent corn was universal but I do remember that it was two or three years before John D. acquired seed for the yellow Hastings Prolific variety. Some of the advertisements for the variety claimed that each stalk of corn would grow up to as many as five ears of corn to a stalk. It was a valid claim as I have seen many stalks with five ears on them. However, most stalks grew only two or three ears of corn.

While discussing the need to protect the teeth of our livestock, cows as well as horses and mules, it is noteworthy to point out that the giant velvet beans which we planted and grew concurrently with our corn were left in the field for the cattle to find and consume often fell down and were trampled under the feet of the cattle. This covered the outside of the hull of the bean pod with gritty sand. We learned that our cattle only three or four years old had worn their teeth to the gums chewing those velvet beans with sand on them.

While the horses and mules did not eat beans, they did eat corn. We had a mule named Pearl which was 22 years old when we got rid of her. Poor thing could not chew corn because her teeth were completely gone. So, she just swallowed the kernels whole.

Vegetatively Propagated Plants

Other crops which we had to grow year after year, but which we could not use seed to grow were sugarcane, Irish potatoes, sweet potatoes and shallots which we called green onions.

The sugarcane plant, which we grew for syrup production, is a grass. In the tropics the plant keeps growing year after year as it does not freeze. There, new stems can be cut off and the sugar recovered. Our latitude in North Louisiana did not permit us to plant the sugarcane from current crop cane as is done in South Louisiana. Hence, we cut some of the cane crop before the first frost came. The first frost around Provencal occurred usually about Thanksgiving to December 1. So, we made it a practice to harvest a portion of the sugarcane to save for planting around November. We buried the stalks in what we called "wind rows" in which the roots and bottoms of the stalks first laid down were covered by the tops of the next bundle of cane, etc. Then around March 15, we dug up the stalks we had buried the preceding November and planted the stalks in our new cane field. After planting in March, the cane was mature enough about October 10 to grind for syrup. This routine went on year after year.

Irish potatoes or white potatoes famously known for use in cooking into "French Fries" are a unique plant. While, technically, the plant does produce seed, it does not produce seed when grown under our crop field conditions. Hence, a different routine was used and is used to grow potatoes. The potato itself is an enlarged portion of an underground stem of the plant. It is commonly called a tuber.

The potatoes themselves are cut into pieces and planted as though each piece were a seed. From this planting new potato plants will grow. Underground the tubers called potatoes will grow and can be dug as the product which again can either be consumed or set aside to be used as "seed" potatoes to grow the next crop. It is really quite simple. We grew two crops of potatoes each year. One we planted about January 15 and dug the potatoes about April. The other crop we planted about September 1 and dug the potatoes about December 1.

If you wish to do so you can grow a potato plant using the described method by burying part of a potato in a pot of soil. Water it and watch it grow for about 90 days and you can dig the new potatoes from under the soil. You may begin that process with any potato from the grocery store. That is a neat project for a little kid needing a science project for school; or just a home project that can be enjoyed by all household members.

A different proposition faces he who wishes to grow some sweet potatoes. We grew sweet potatoes in large areas during the great depression. Sometimes we planted as much as three acres. They are good for human consumption. And, they are good for feeding cattle and hogs. When boiled they are good for feeding chickens.

The portion of the sweet potato plant that we eat is the root. I understand from literature that sometimes the leaves are cooked and consumed. That was not practiced at the Sylvest homestead.

One feature of sweet potatoes is that as food for hogs, the potatoes do not have to be harvested. That is, they do not have to be dug up and cured. Hogs and sweet potatoes go together well as complementary enterprises. The hogs can go into the field of sweet potatoes and root them out and consume them, saving the manual labor of digging and storing the potatoes.

When the potatoes are exhausted and the hogs are fat, the butchering process can take place. By that time, in early winter, the temperatures are low enough to encourage the killing of the hogs. Hence, the term we often used around Provencal, "Hog Killing Weather." Cold weather took the place of refrigeration which we did not have without electricity.

Propagation of the sweet potato is a bit more complicated than that for Irish potatoes. In late winter or early spring sweet potatoes were placed in a cold frame, or hotbed with several inches of well tilled soil. The potatoes are laid nearly touching each other in a single layer. A light layer of soil is used to cover the potatoes. The cover to the cold frame is put into place. That cover was often discarded glass windows so the warmth of the sun could penetrate the glass and heat the atmosphere inside the cold frame encouraging the growth of the sprouts on the sweet potatoes. After a few days, up to a few weeks in the early Spring, the sweet potatoes produce an abundance of sprouting young plants. When the sprouts are about a foot long they are broken loose from the potato. The sprouts are ready for transplanting into the field where the new sweet potato crop is to grow. A lot of hand labor is required. Such is the vegetative process for the sweet potatoes, since, being a biennial plant, it does not produce seed under our crop growing conditions.

Old Blue

Subsistence living in the piney woods during The Great Depression was necessarily connected to the hog. The hog was the primary source of fat in the human diet. The number of people to be fed at any homestead determined, to a great extent, the number of hogs produced for consumption in the household.

Two households only one and one-half miles apart, each with two parents and thirteen children required large numbers of hogs. These were the Kay and the Sylvest families in this story.

Open range was the norm because the land was poor and larger amounts of land were needed to provide the food for hogs which would travel for miles on the open range in search of anything edible.

In the management of this resource, each homesteader had his arrangement for breeding, growing, butchering and preserving the meat and fat from his hogs.

A.G. Kay known as "Pink," was a large man about six feet five inches tall. He and Lottie Cobb Kay, his wife, kept hogs on the open range and raised corn in their fenced in fields on which to feed the hogs to fatten them for butchering. The Kay farm was about four miles south of Provencal, LA. Mr. Kay not only lived in a log cabin; he had a log corn crib and a log smoke house for curing the meat. The Sylvest homestead where I lived was similarly equipped though not a log cabin.

Mr. Kay had a hog dog named Jack that really was the envy of hog owners for miles around. I have often heard, as a child, that Pink had refused over one hundred dollars for that dog, an unheard of price at the time for a dog. John D.'s hog dog was named "Ring," and he was good, though no real competition for Jack.

Each year the sows of the respective herds of hogs which ranged together produced a brood of pigs in the spring and another brood in the fall. Each family had about three sows which were relied upon to produce pigs to replace those butchered or sold. Some of the brood sows continued to produce pigs annually for years.

The most famous of these was a sow owned by Pink named "Old Blue." I thought that Old Blue was a witch, because that is what she turned out to be to all the neighbors except her owner, Pink, who deemed her his best and most productive brood sow. She was really the mother of his herd. She was born before 1935, because when I was ten years old I met her as the unseen robber of our cornfield.

All the farmers of the neighborhood had trouble keeping neighborhood hogs from breaking through their fences and eating their corn. A hog was breaking through our fence every time we repaired it. It was my assignment to chase the offending swine back through the fence where it had entered and repair the fence. I became good at my task but the fence was not hog proof. It simply was not strong enough to keep the champion fence breaking hog of all time out of our field of corn. That field must have tasted awfully good to the offending swine because it seemed to me that it was his or her favorite corn patch.

Pink Kay died about a year after I met Old Blue, about 1936. Of course, the ownership of Old Blue simply passed on to Lottie, Mrs Kay. The practical daily management of Old Blue and her kind passed to my friend and classmate, James Kay, son of Pink and Lottie, as James was the oldest son at home.

At the time Pink died I had not yet identified the ghost of a hog that was so effective at making his or her entrances through our cornfield fence. I had chased that hog for about three years with Ring. However, as the hog is a very wary animal, it was hard for a pursuing boy of my age to see and identify the culprit.

On more than one occasion in the late thirties, James Kay and I had hunted our hogs together. That is, we went into the nearby woods, located the Kay brood sows, ear marked their pigs with the Pink Kay mark, an over-slope and under-bit in each ear. If we located any of John D.'s hogs we marked the pigs with the Sylvest earmark, an upper half crop in each ear and an under-bit in the left ear.

I recall helping James Kay catch and mark a brood of baby pigs produced by Old Blue. The bed of pine straw she had assembled as a warm safe spot to conceal her pigs was on a hillside halfway between the Kay and the Sylvest homesteads. James and I caught and earmarked nine baby pigs with the Kay earmark. We castrated the male pigs of the litter as the custom was.

It was about 1939 or 1940 before I found out that the primary hog that was breaking through the fence to our corn was Old Blue. The way that happened is one of the most fascinating bits of animal ingenuity I have ever observed. I had Ring on the trail of the hog eating our corn and we were close to the game. It had rained the night before and the water in McKims Creek was about two feet above normal with flooding rainwater. I had been totally unable to find where the culprit hog had entered the field. I could find no hole in the fence. Fortunately, I was standing next to where the fence crossed McKims Creek when the chase approached. I stood totally still so I would not frighten the hog, hoping I would get a look at the thief.

Sure enough, Old Blue came right by me, stopped, not seeing me, but probably smelling me, took a look around, dived into the muddy water that was about four feet deep, swam under water for about ten feet and came up out of the water on the other side of the fence. Not only had I identified the thief but I had located the hole in the fence. My eyes must have almost popped out of my head. I had never seen such a caper.

Each place the fence crosses a flowing stream a water gap of sorts must be built in the fence so the water can get through without destroying the fence. By the next day the water in McKims Creek had fallen back to normal. I went to the fence and saw the hole in the hog wire in the water gap where Old Blue had gone through underwater.

I was disappointed that most people to whom I told the story did not believe it. I never told James this story. It was the responsibility of each homesteader living in the open range to fence his property in such a manner that his crops were protected from all free ranging animals. It would have been embarrassing to admit that you could not build and maintain such a fence, even to keep an expert experienced fence breaker like Old Blue out of your cornfield.

By that time, Old Blue was indeed getting old. Old Blue also had a reputation. She had eventually been identified as the peskiest fence breaker by nearly all the neighbors. Old Blue ravaged the fences and cornfields of the Kays, Foshees, McGaskeys, Longinos, Honeycutts and Sylvests.

I heard the story that someone had told James that he was going to shoot Old Blue and that James had replied, "If you do, I'll shoot your best cow." I can't verify that part of the story. However, no one, but no one, ever considered shooting anyone's best brood sow let alone their best cow.

I can verify this. The next butchering season Old Blue was put into the fattening pen, fattened up and made into bacon. James would not own a fence breaking hog just like his father, Pink, would not own a goat killing dog (read my book Collard Greens).

My best friend, James Kay, just like his father, believed that being a good neighbor was more important than any animal he owned.

Old Blue probably produced well over a hundred pigs in her lifetime of seven years or so. We all knew that she was one heck of a brood sow. But, it took the neighbors a long time to determine that that ingenuous pig was a heck of a champion fence-breaker as well.

Peace returned to the corn fields around Provencal and Vowells Mill, La. about 1941 with the passing of Old Blue around the breakfast table of the Kay household to be enjoyed as "bacon with biscuits."

Building a Log Church

(Compiled from notes contained in the autobiography of Reverend Spurgeon J. Sylvest, brother to this author)

The Mt. Nebo Baptist Church building was built on an acre of land donated to the church by John D. Sylvest, my father. Reverend Spurgeon J. Sylvest, one of my older brothers became 18 years old in 1932 when I became seven years old.

Spurgeon and Frank Sylvest, another of my four brothers, lived on the Sylvest homestead in 1932. As that residence was located approximately equidistant, about five miles, from Bellwood Baptist Church, Provencal

Baptist Church and Harmony Baptist Church, Spurgeon proposed to his parents that they found a church and build the church building of logs on the Sylvest homestead property. In this way, nearby families who could not walk or ride a wagon the required five miles to attend those distant churches on Sunday would have a place within walking distance of their homes to attend church

Upon agreement to found and build, Spurgeon and Frank built the log cabin almost exclusively with some help from Jefferson Masters and Elbert Foshee and limited amounts of labor from others. I remember helping with the construction.

As a child, I watched as the pine poles were cut and peeled by the older ones. I remember leading a small brown mule, named Jane, snaking the poles from the surrounding woods on the homestead to the site of the building.

I accompanied my older family members as they hauled, by wagon, the 30 inch blocks of "sinker heart cypress" cut and dug out of a cypress break about four miles from the homestead in Santa Barb Creek bottom.

During the summer of 1932, all the members of the family spent all available time splitting the cypress blocks into bolts of wood from which were rived cypress boards, about 3/8 to one-half inch thick, to be trimmed with a hatchet, half-hatchet, foot adz or draw-knife. They were thus fashioned into roofing shingles to be nailed to four-inch lathes as roofing. Rafters were made of small pine poles about three inches in diameter. A hipped roof covered the four extensions of the floor plan design which was in the shape of a cross. There were 10,000 roofing boards rived out, trimmed for roofing the building and neatly stacked at the building site.

I do not have the precise dimensions nor design of the floor plan nor elevation drawings. John D., a finished carpenter and builder, designed and directed the entire church building project. I am confident there were no drawings made from which to work.

I watched the entire process from a kingbird seat, old enough to observe and help, but not yet capable of handling, and not expected to handle, an adult assignment during the process.

I brought cold water from the well to laborers on the project, handed material to adults and took chores around the farm so adults could work on the building.

From notes contained in the autobiography of Rev. Spurgeon J. Sylvest, I am able to share some of his memories of the time.

He stated that the building was built mostly on Saturdays. On week days Spurgeon was attending school at Provencal and Frank was working in the fields growing a crop for John D. and other family members.

By 1933 the church building was nearly completed and some pews had been built.

The cost of the entire project, according to Spurgeon's writings, was $28, which was spent purchasing two used doors and four used windows plus nails.

The foundation of the building was formed of red stones dug from a nearby gravel pit. On these stones, heart pine blocks were placed. Heart pine logs used as sills were placed on the blocks.

The flooring joists were of peeled pine poles upon which the log pen was built to form the walls. A hip design for the roof without exposed gables minimized the lengths of the rafters as well as the roofing material, which, in turn, strengthened the entire structure.

Timber cut from the homestead by Frank and Spurgeon was traded to a sawmill about four miles from the homestead in exchange for sawing and hauling logs and lumber.

Some of the lumber was likewise exchanged for similar services by a planing mill, which, I believe, was located near Natchitoches, LA. The planed lumber was used for construction of the pulpit and the pews in the form of benches with backs. The bench pews were portable.

Rough sawed one by fours were used as lathes nailed to the pole rafters. Rough sawed one by six inch pine lumber became the floors.

The building was heated by a, Benjamin Franklin type, wood burning heater in the very middle of the floor. The pipe had a damper fitted into the stove pipe. The damper was quite effective in controlling the speed with which the wood burned in the stove, thereby controlling the output of heat from the heater along with the amount of wood fed to the fire. The exhaust from the heater went straight up through the roof overhead.

The cracks between the logs in the walls were filled with red clay mixed with Spanish moss and/or pine straw. Then, cypress boards cut in lengths of about six to ten feet were rived from logs of heart cypress and individually cut to fit as interior ceiling on the walls.

The two years following the completion of the church building in 1933, we continued to rive boards until we had enough to cover our boxed in house. The entire roof on the house required 8,000 boards, some of which were as wide as twelve inches.

The building continued to be used as Mt. Nebo Baptist Church until John D. and Minnie Sylvest sold their farm and moved from the homestead to Baton Rouge, LA about 1951.

I attended Mt. Nebo, led singing and taught Sunday School classes to younger children until I graduated from high school in 1942 and left home to go to work and attend college at Louisiana State University in Baton Rouge.

I have not learned what happened to the building, but believe it was given to someone who hauled it elsewhere sometime in the 1950s.

Fire in the Piney Woods

When I referred to the hazards of fire in one of the chapters of these volumes I was asked for more detail. Now, this chapter begins.

Upon arrival at their new home on Sylvest Road near Provencal after dark, the first adventure was with the hog lice contained in the straw which ten and twelve year old boys stole from the range hog's bed in the dark.

The next was preparing breakfast for two adults and seven children without a stove. Fireplace it was.

First inspection of the house in 1922 revealed that it had two fireplaces with mud chimneys, one in the living room at the end of one of the separately gabled sections of the house and the other at the end of the kitchen-dining room portion.

Boxes of safety matches were available at the stores in Provencal for five cents. A box of matches contained about two hundred matches. Since fires had to be built daily during the warmer months of the year, the need for matches and kindling was daily. A box of matches was kept on the mantlepiece in the living room and in the kitchen above the fireplaces.

As fires were a tool in destroying tree parts resulting from clearing of land, the men typically carried matches in their pockets so they could be used whenever the need arose. Members of most families smoked. Pipes, cigarettes rolled by hand, and cigarettes in packages already rolled, termed "ready rolls," were another reason for men to carry matches at all times.

The countryside was endless rolling hills with creeks and branches in between. Those hills had just had harvested from them the virgin pine timber which had first been tapped by the turpentine crews, one of which was just completing the dismantling of their camp one quarter mile east of the Sylvest property on what is now designated the Eric Miller Road.

The turpentine workers had a pet mule which my father acquired as a trade of sorts. The baby mule had lost its mother so had been raised on cows milk from a bottle. The family named the mule Jane.

As the turpentine camp was being torn down and the workers and their families were departing, they burned much of what they could not carry with them. Soon the railroads which had been built to haul logs from the virgin pine forest to the sawmills were loaded on the last trains out as the tracks were pulled from the cross ties and hauled away to be used in building tracks elsewhere as needed.

All of the burning that occurred was subject to setting the old refuse from the timber harvesting on fire. There were patches which were only partially burned leaving spots of partially burned pine limbs, particularly the knots which had not burned completely. Along with that refuse, the new undergrowth plants of all kinds, trees, shrubs, and grass were burned on what appeared to be about an annual basis.

Uncontrolled fires like these we called woods fires.

The 1920s predated the founding of the Kisatchie National Forest and the fire protection towers that the US Forest Service constructed in the 1930s. So, when forest fires burned, there were few people and limited resources dedicated to control of fires in the woods. Homeowners were on their own.

I remember riding the school bus to Provencal on school days and when the bus would go over hills, with virtually no large trees obscuring the view, if there was a fire in the woods within five miles we could see the smoke. Sometimes such fires would burn for weeks before a heavy rain came along and extinguished them.

Some homes were located closer to patches of new forest which were subject to catching fire because of dense growths of grass underneath the trees. When one of these homes was threatened by the approach of a burning woods fire, the owner would notify his neighbors and solicit help in fighting the approaching fire.

When I was nine years old in 1935 we had a severe drought in Louisiana as well as across the United States. That was the year of the dust bowl. A woods fire was burning about two miles south of our fence. Our south fence which ran east and west was directly in the path of the fire.

John D. had ridden on Jane, his best saddle mule, to assess the risk of the fire. His conclusion, we must go fight the fire or it is going to burn our fence and our woods.

Older brothers got the middle buster with a rolling coulter which, pulled by two draft animals, can plow a wide furrow which would help stop a grass fire moving across the woods under the trees.

While our fence along that half-mile property line on the South side was of galvanized hog wire 32 inches high, topped with two barbed wires, the wire would not burn. However, the fence posts were of fat pine and they would burn most easily. We had to save that fence. Additionally, if the wire was exposed fully to the fire the heat destroyed the galvanized coating that prevented rust.

Frank and Spurgeon took two mules and the plow and plowed a furrow the best they could along that fence. That was in the edge of our woods, not an open field. Hence, there was an abundance of small tree roots which interfered with the plowing. Many spots the plow could not penetrate the ground at all. However, it opened a strip elsewhere that could be used along with additional clearing by hoe, rake and shovel at the fighting line to stop the fire.

I was too young and small to be allowed to help with the described heavy work during the night. However, when daybreak came my mother prepared food, put it in a container and sent me a half mile into the woods to find Papa, Frank and Spurgeon and bring them food and water.

I took a gallon jug and filled it at a spring nearby which we kept clear for drinking water. I took the jug back to the workers. A gallon jug of water weighs 8 pounds and is a good load for a seventy-pound spindly-legged ten-year old.

The fire had approached in several spots. Fence posts were on fire. Despite that, our efforts kept the fire from burning all the posts in the fence, saving most of them. I helped put out the fires along the fence. My father taught me how to select a pine limb on a young pine tree the right size to break off and using the limb for a handle beat the fire out with the green pine straw.

You can bet one little kid had tall tales about fighting a woods fire to tell to his friends. Such events were common in the piney woods.

There was a young school teacher teaching at some of the local schools of Natchitoches Parish in the 1920s named Caroline Dorman who was so concerned about the forests of Natchitoches Parish and the rest of the region that she is said to have conducted a tireless campaign at the federal level to convince Congress and the presidents to found Kisatchie National Forest. Miss Dorman taught school at Kisatchie High School, about ten miles from my home at the same time as my sister, Dixie Sylvest Moss.

The Caroline Dorman Nature Preserve in Saline, LA in northeast Natchitoches Parish honors her efforts and memory.

I remember when the National Forest Service planted the traditional sign with the federal medallion denoting the entrance to that region of Kisatchie National Forest shortly after it was established in 1930. The sign was placed about a mile south of Provencal on LA 117 (LA 39 at the time) on the West side of the road. Nearby, the school bus I rode picked up the Luther Moss and Buck Ballard children.

Woods fires were exciting events and provided much entertainment to school age children, while giving agony to some of their parents. Occasionally a house or barn would catch on fire from woods fires, especially when the wind was blowing.

When woods fires burned the woods they left huge acreages, sometimes miles of denuded ground. Not all of the timber burned in the woods fires. Only when the underbrush grass, debris from downed trees was very dense did the fire become hot enough to kill older timber a few or more inches in diameter.

As the years went by and the second-growth forests grew larger, more mature trees and as woods fires were controlled by the forest service through fire prevention and forest management programs, the problems with woods fires were lessened. Now, more descriptively called forest fires, they have declined in frequency and in danger to threatened landowners.

There were some side effects of woods fires due to the open range policies of the times.

When a woods fire left the range denuded, as soon as the rains returned to the area and the growing season began, the grass that germinated from the many seed that were not burned by the fire produced a green carpet appearance when viewed from near the ground. Such a view of the sparse green grass a few inches high virtually intoxicated the cattle on the open range deluding them into thinking they were entering a dense green growth in which they could graze. Their eyes viewed the sparse grass from a few inches above the ground and they went berserk running to the next patch only to discover that there was no grass there on which to graze either.

When a burn occurred near enough to our range area for our livestock to see it and visit it, we rounded up our cattle and put them in the pasture to keep them from running themselves into heavy weight loss and damaging their health.

This characteristic amused us as school children but it did not amuse our parents and those who owned cattle on the open range.

The development of the Forest Service programs diminished the threats of fires of all kinds in the piney woods. Power vehicles and equipment became the norm. Fire lookout towers enabled fires to be discovered before they spread to such a size that they could not be put out with ease.

Then, along came airplanes and helicopters reducing risks even further. In the 1920s and 1930s we could only imagine such things.

Times and fires have changed. Many homes do not have a match to be found.

Author's Timeline

1923 J. D. Sylvest purchases homestead and moves to Provencal, LA area.

1925 Author, Thomas Ard Sylvest, born.

1931 Author enters first grade at Provencal School

1941 Japanese attack Pearl Harbor

1942 Author graduates from provencal High School
Author enters LSU

1944 Author enters US Army Air Corps

1945 August, Japans surrenders, WWII ends

1946 February, Author returns to Provencal
September, Author reenters LSU

1949 Author earns BS degree at LSU

Pictures and Maps

Provencal High School

Vowell's Mill School

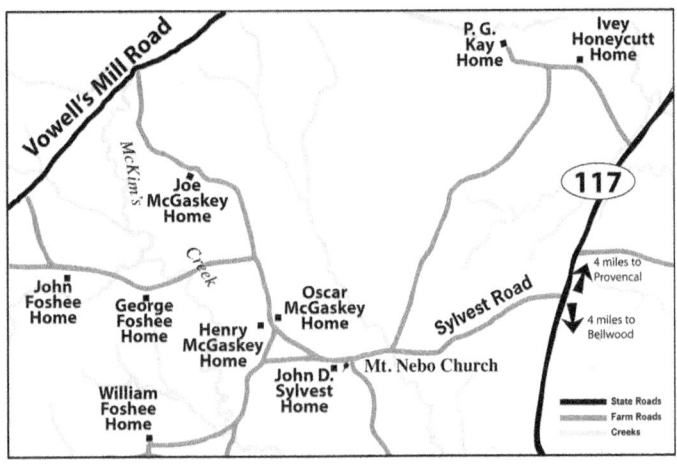

Buttermilk

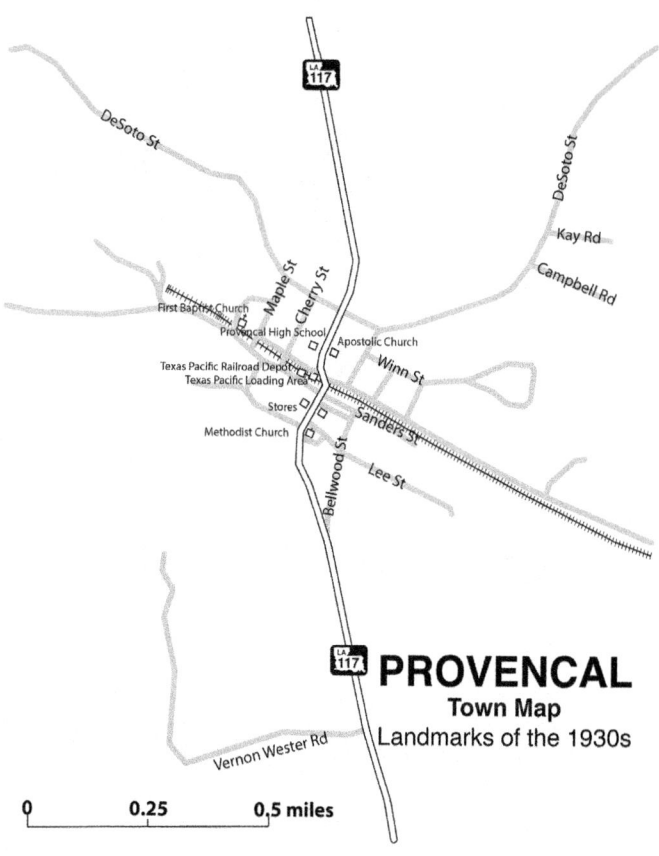

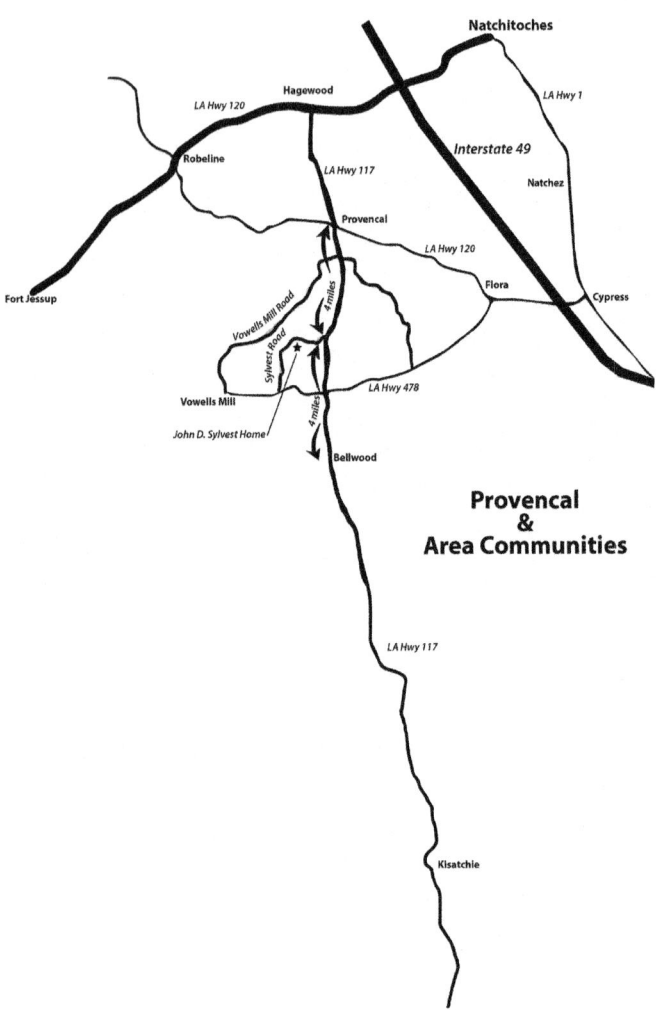

CPSIA information can be obtained at www.ICGtesting.com
Printed in the USA
BVOW08s1915270716
457091BV00001B/6/P